STEP-BY-STEP

Low Fat Baking

Low Fat Baking

Carole Handslip

Photography by Amanda Heywood

SMITHMARK

© Anness Publishing Limited 1996

This edition published in 1996
by SMITHMARK Publishers, a division of US Media Holdings, Inc.
16 East 32nd Street
New York
NY 10016
USA

SMITHMARK Books are available for bulk purchase
for sales promotion and for premium use. For details write or call the
Manager of Special Sales, SMITHMARK Publishers,
16 East 32nd Street, New York, NY 10016; (212) 532-6600

Produced by Anness Publishing Limited
1 Boundary Row
London SE1 8HP

ISBN 0 7651 9756 1

Publisher: Joanna Lorenz
Senior Cookery Editor: Linda Fraser
Assistant Editor: Emma Brown
Designer: Alan Marshall
Photographer: Amanda Heywood

Printed and bound in Hong Kong

CONTENTS

Introduction	6
Techniques	16
SMALL TREATS	22
CAKES	36
SAVORY BUNS AND BISCUITS	48
BREADS	60
SPECIAL OCCASION CAKES	82
Index	96

INTRODUCTION

It is generally agreed that a high fat diet is bad for us, especially if the fats are of the saturated variety. Unless you are making meringues or angel food cake, it is rarely possible to do entirely without fat in baking. However, it is possible to cut down considerably on the amount of fat used, and equally good results can be achieved using unsaturated oils instead of saturated fats.

Polyunsaturated oils such as sunflower oil, corn oil and safflower oil are excellent for most baking purposes, but choose olive oil, which is monounsaturated, for recipes that require a good, strong flavor. When an oil is unsuitable, a margarine which is high in polyunsaturates is the fat to choose. Low fat spreads are ideal for spreading but not good for baking, since they contain a high proportion of water.

Although cheese is high in saturated fat, its flavor makes it invaluable in many recipes. Choose reduced-fat varieties with a mature flavor, or much less of a highly flavored cheese such as Parmesan. When using less fat, you can add extra moisture to cakes and quick breads in the form of fresh or dried fruits. There is no need to use whole milk – try skim milk or fruit juice instead. Buttermilk (the liquid leftover from churning butter) is, surprisingly, virtually fat free and is perfect for soda bread and biscuits. Cream undoubtedly adds a touch of luxury to special occasion cakes, however, low fat ricotta cheese, thick yogurt or cottage cheese sweetened with honey make delicious, low fat fillings and toppings for even the most elaborate cakes.

So you will see that using less fat doesn't prevent you from making scrumptious cakes and cookies that look and taste every bit as good as those made with butter and cream. The recipes in this book are sure to inspire, impress and amaze anyone who believed low fat baking was too good to be true.

Pantry

Many of the most useful and important baking ingredients are found in the pantry. The following guide highlights a few of the most essential items.

FLOURS

Mass-produced, highly refined flours are fine for most baking purposes, but for the very best results choose organic stone-ground flours because they will add flavor as well as texture to your baking.

Bread flour

Made from hard wheat, which contains a high proportion of gluten, this flour is the one to use for bread making.

Cake or pastry flour

This fine-textured flour contains less gluten and more starch than all-purpose flour. Use for light cakes and cookies.

Whole-wheat flour

Because this flour contains the complete wheat kernel, it gives a coarser texture and a good wholesome flavor to bread.

Rye flour

This dark-colored flour has a low gluten content and gives a dense, dark loaf with a good flavor. It is best mixed with bread flour to give a lighter loaf.

NUTS

Most nuts are low in saturated fats and high in polyunsaturated fats. Use them sparingly, since their total fat content is high.

HERBS AND SPICES

Chopped fresh herbs add interest and flavor to baking. In the absence of fresh herbs, dried herbs can be used: less is needed but the flavor is generally not as good.

Spices can add either strong or subtle flavors depending on the amount and variety used. Ground cinnamon and nutmeg are among the most useful for baking, but more exotic spices, such as saffron or cardomom, can also be used to great effect.

SWEETENERS

Unrefined sugars

Most baking recipes call for sugar. Choose unrefined sugar, rather than refined sugars, as they have more flavor and contain some minerals.

Honey

Good honey has a strong flavor so you can use rather less of it than the equivalent amount of sugar. It also contains traces of minerals and vitamins.

Malt extract

This is a sugary by-product of barley, which is available in most health food stores. It has a strong flavor and is good to use in bread, cakes and quick breads as it adds a moistness of its own.

Molasses

This is the residue from the first stage of refining sugar cane. It has a strong, smoky and slightly bitter taste, which gives a good flavor to cookies and cakes. Black treacle can often be used as a substitute for molasses.

Fruit juice

Concentrated fruit juices are very useful for baking. They have no added sweeteners or preservatives and can be diluted as required. Use them in their concentrated form for baking or for sweetening fillings.

Pear and apple spread

This is a very concentrated fruit juice with no added sugar. It has a sweet-sour taste and can be used as a spread or blended with a little fruit juice and added to baking recipes as a sweetener. It is available in most health food stores.

Dried fruits

These are a traditional addition to cakes and quick breads and there is a very wide range available, including more unusual varieties such as peach, pineapple, banana, mango and papaya. The natural sugars add sweetness to baked goods and keep them moist, making it possible to use less fat.

cracked wheat   olives   flour

bottled apricots

dried pineapple   dried yeast

eggs

light brown su

currants *poppy seeds* *honey* *herbs*

fresh fruit *oatmeal* *cinnamon sticks* *dried apricots* *sesame seeds*

chestnuts *sunflower s* *physalis* *linseed*

raisins *candied cherries* *olive oil* *pear and apple spread* *apricot compôte* *dates*

garlic *extra virgin olive oil* *fresh fruit*

rolled oats *orange juice* *semolina*

Oils, Fats and Dairy Produce

OILS AND FATS

Low fat spreads are ideal for using on breads and quick breads, but are unfortunately not suitable for baking, because they have a high water content.

When you are baking, try to avoid saturated fats such as butter and hard margarine, and use oils high in polyunsaturates such as sunflower, corn or safflower oil. When margarine is essential, choose a variety which is high in polyunsaturates.

Reduced-fat butter

This contains about 40% fat; the rest is water and milk solids emulsified together. It is not suitable for baking.

Low fat spread, rich buttermilk blend

Made with a high proportion of buttermilk, which is naturally low in fat. Unsuitable for baking.

Sunflower light

Not suitable for baking, since it contains only 40% fat, plus emulsified water and milk solids.

Olive oil reduced-fat spread

Based on olive oil, this spread has a better flavor than some other low fat spreads, but it is unsuitable for baking.

Very low fat spread

Contains only 20–30% fat, and so is unsuitable for baking.

Olive oil

Use this monounsaturated oil when a recipe requires a good, strong flavor. It is best to use extra virgin olive oil.

Sunflower oil

High in polyunsaturates, this is the oil used most frequently in this book, since it has a pleasant but not too dominant flavor.

LOW FAT CHEESES

There are a lot of low fat cheeses that can be used in baking. Generally, harder cheeses have a higher fat content than soft cheeses. Choose mature cheese if possible, since you need less of it to get a good flavor.

Cottage cheese

A low fat soft cheese that is also available in a reduced-fat form.

Soft curd farmer cheese

Made from fermented skim milk, this soft, white cheese is virtually free of fat.

Nonfat cream cheese

This has a slightly softer texture than full fat cream cheese. It can be used as a lower fat substitute for the full fat variety.

Feta cheese

This is a medium fat cheese with a firm, crumbly texture. It has a slightly sour, salty flavor which can range from bland to strong.

Mozzarella light
This is a medium fat version of an Italian soft cheese.

Edam and Maasdam
Two medium fat hard cheeses.

Half-fat cheddar and Red Leicester
These contain about 14% fat.

CREAM ALTERNATIVES
Yogurt, low fat ricotta cheese and nonfat cream cheese make excellent alternatives to cream, and when combined with honey, liqueurs or other flavorings, they make delicious fillings or toppings for cakes and cookies.

Low fat ricotta cheese
This is a fresh, white, moist cheese. It is usually made from whey and skim milk.

Crème fraîche
This is easy to make at home by mixing 1 cup whipping cream with 2 tablespoons buttermilk. Cover and leave at room temperature until very thick.

Light and nonfat sour cream
Light sour cream contains about 40% less fat than regular sour cream. Nonfat sour cream is, of course, lower in fat.

Yogurt
Plain and flavored yogurts can be used in place of cream. Low fat yogurt contains about 1% fat.

Strained plain yogurt
This thick, creamy yogurt, made from whole milk, has a fat content of 10%. A low fat version is also available.

semi-skim milk

buttermilk

low fat yogurt

strained plain yogurt

eggs

light sour cream

low fat ricotta cheese

LOW FAT MILKS

Skim milk
This milk has had virtually all fat removed, leaving 0.1–0.3%. It is ideal for those wishing to cut down their fat intake.

Semi-skim milk
With a fat content of only 1.5–1.8%, this milk tastes less rich than whole milk. It is favored by many people for everyday use for precisely this reason.

Powdered skim milk
A useful, low fat standby.

Buttermilk
Made from skim milk with a bacterial culture added. It is very low in fat.

Equipment

Baking sheet
Choose a large, heavy baking sheet that will not warp at high temperatures.

Balloon whisk
Perfect for whisking egg whites and incorporating air into other light mixtures.

Box grater
This multipurpose grater can be used for citrus rind, fruit and vegetables, and cheese.

Brown paper
Used for wrapping around the outside of cake pans to protect the cake mixture from the full heat of the oven.

Cake tester
A simple implement, which, when inserted into a cooked cake, will come out clean if the cake is ready.

Cook's knife
This has a heavy, wide blade, and is ideal for chopping.

Deep round cake pan
This deep pan is ideal for baking fruit cakes.

Electric whisk
Very useful for creaming cake mixtures, whipping cream, and whisking egg whites.

Honey twirl
For spooning honey without making a mess!

Jelly roll pan
This shallow pan is designed especially for jelly rolls.

Juicer
Made from porcelain, glass or plastic – used for squeezing the juice from citrus fruits.

Loaf pan
Available in various sizes, and used for making loaf-shaped breads and quick breads.

Measuring cup
Essential for measuring any kind of liquid accurately.

Measuring spoons
Standard measuring spoons are essential for measuring small quantities of ingredients.

Metal spoons
Large metal spoons are perfect for folding, since they minimize the amount of air that escapes.

Mixing bowls
A set of different-sized bowls is essential in any kitchen for whisking, mixing, and so on.

Muffin pan
Shaped into individual cups, this pan is much simpler to use than individual paper cases. It can also be used for baking small pies and tarts.

Nutmeg grater
This miniature grater is used for grating whole nutmegs.

Nylon sifter
Suitable for most baking purposes, and particularly for sifting foods that react adversely with metal.

Parchment paper
For lining pans and baking sheets to ensure that cakes, and cookies do not stick.

Pastry brush
Useful for brushing excess flour from pastry and brushing glazes over pastries, breads and tarts.

Pastry cutters
Used for stamping out pastry, cookies and biscuits.

Rectangular cake pan
For making cakes that are served cut into slices.

Ring mold
Ideal for making angel food cake and other ring-shaped cakes.

Scissors
Vital for cutting paper and snipping dough and pastry.

Spatula
Used to loosen pies, tarts and breads from baking sheets, and to smooth icing over cakes.

Spongecake pan
Ideal for spongecakes. Make sure you have two of them.

Square cake pan
Used for making square cakes, or cakes served cut into squares.

Vegetable knife
A useful knife for preparing a variety of fruit and vegetables.

Wire rack
Ideal for cooling cakes and cookies, allowing circulation of air to prevent sogginess.

Wire mesh strainer
A large, wire mesh strainer is ideal for most baking purposes.

Wooden spoon
Essential for mixing ingredients, and creaming mixtures.

rectangular cake pan

square cake pan

baking sheet

balloon whisk

large metal spoon *wooden spoon*

electric whisk

mixing bowls

parchment paper

brown paper

scissors

spongecake pan

pastry brush

ring mold

cake tester

measuring cup

wire rack

pastry cutters

deep round cake pan

vegetable knife

honey twirl

wire rack

jelly roll tin

juicer

wire mesh strainer

nutmeg grater

cook's knife

spatulas

box grater

nylon sifter

measuring spoons

muffin pan

Facts about Fats

Most of us eat far more fat every day than the ¼ oz that our bodies need; on average we each consume about 4 oz fat each day.

Current nutritional advice isn't quite that strict on fat intake though, and it suggests that we should limit our daily intake to no more than 30% of total calories. In real terms, this means that for an average intake of 2,000 calories a day, 30% of energy would come from about 600 calories. Since each ounce of fat provides 240 calories, your total daily intake should be no more than 2½ oz fat.

It's easy to cut down on obvious sources of fat such as butter, margarine, cream, whole milk and high fat cheeses, but watch out for "hidden" fats. Although we may think of cakes and cookies as sweet foods, more calories come from their fat than from their sugar. Indeed, of the quarter of our fat intake that comes from non-meat sources, a fifth comes from dairy products and margarine and the rest from cakes, cookies, pastries and other foods. The merits of low fat baking are enormous, since you can cut down on your fat intake in general, and also control exactly how much fat you and your family consume, and the type of fat it is.

Fats can be divided into two main categories – saturated and unsaturated. We are all well aware of the dangers of saturated fats in relation to blocking arteries and causing coronary heart disease. Much of the saturated fat we eat comes from animal sources – meat and dairy products such as suet and butter – that are solid at room temperature. However, there are also some saturated fats of vegetable origin, most notably coconut and palm oils. In addition, some margarines are "hydrogenated" – a process which increases the proportion of saturated fat they contain. These margarines should be avoided.

Unsaturated fats can be divided into two main types: monounsaturated and polyunsaturated. Mono-unsaturated fats are found in various foods including olive oil, rapeseed oil and some nuts. These fats may actually help lower blood cholesterol, and this could explain why in Mediterranean countries, where olive oil is widely consumed, there is such a low incidence of heart disease.

The polyunsaturated fats most familiar to us are of vegetable or plant origin, and include sunflower oil, corn oil, soy oil, walnut oil and many margarines. It was believed at one time, that it was beneficial to switch to polyunsaturated fats, since they may also help lower cholesterol. Today, however, most experts believe that it is more important to reduce the total intake of all kinds of fat.

Above: *Animal products such as suet, butter and some margarines are major sources of saturated fats.*

Left: *Some oils, such as olive and rapeseed, are thought to help lower blood cholesterol.*

Right: *Vegetable and plant oils and some margarines are high in polyunsaturated fat.*

The Fat and Calorie Contents of Food

This chart shows the weight of fat and the energy content of 4 oz (115g) of various foods.

FRUIT AND NUTS	Fat (g)	Calories
Apples, eating	0.1	47
Avocados	19.5	190
Bananas	0.3	95
Dried mixed fruit	1.6	227
Grapefruit	0.1	30
Oranges	0.1	37
Peaches	0.1	33
Almonds	55.8	612
Brazil nuts	68.2	682
Peanut butter, smooth	53.7	623
Pine nuts	68.6	688

DAIRY PRODUCE, FATS AND OILS	Fat (g)	Calories
Cream, heavy	48.0	449
Cream, light	19.1	198
Cream, whipping	39.3	373
Milk, skim	0.1	33
Milk, whole	3.9	66
Cheddar cheese	34.4	412
Cheddar-type, reduced-fat	15.0	261
Cream cheese	47.4	439
Brie	26.9	319
Edam cheese	25.4	333
Feta cheese	20.2	250
Parmesan cheese	32.7	452
Low fat yogurt, plain	0.8	56
Strained plain yogurt	9.1	115
Butter	81.7	737
Lard	99.0	891
Low fat spread	40.5	390
Margarine	81.6	739
Coconut oil	99.9	899
Corn oil	99.9	899
Olive oil	99.9	899J
Safflower oil	99.9	899
Eggs (2, small)	10.9	147
Egg white	Trace	36
Egg yolk	30.5	339

OTHER FOODS	Fat (g)	Calories
Sugar	0	94
Chocolate, milk	30.3	529
Honey	0	88
Jam	0	61
Marmalade	0	61
Lemon curd	5.1	283

TECHNIQUES

Using Yeast

There are three main types of yeast currently available – dried, rapid-rise and fresh. Rapid-rise is added directly to the dry ingredients, whereas dried and fresh yeast must first be mixed with warm liquid and a little sugar to activate them.

USING DRIED YEAST

1 Measure dried yeast, then sprinkle it into the warm liquid in a cup or small bowl with a pinch of sugar. Stir well, and set aside in a warm place for about 10–15 minutes.

COOK'S TIP

Dried yeast doesn't dissolve well in milk. You must either leave it for about 30 minutes to froth, or if you are in a hurry, dissolve it in a little water first.

2 When the yeast liquid becomes frothy, stir it into the dry ingredients.

USING RAPID-RISE YEAST

1 Add rapid-rise yeast to the dry ingredients directly from the package. Do not dissolve it in liquid first.

COOK'S TIP

Rapid-rise yeast is a special kind of dried yeast with a fine grain – it raises bread in as little as half the normal time. Bread made with this kind of yeast can be shaped after mixing, and given only one rising.

USING FRESH YEAST

1 Place fresh yeast in a small bowl with a pinch of sugar, and a little lukewarm water. Cream together until smooth, then set aside for 5–10 minutes until frothy, before adding to the dry ingredients.

Shaping Rolls

Bread rolls can be made in all sorts of interesting shapes and sizes. Begin by dividing the dough into even-size portions.

1 To make cottage rolls, divide each portion of dough into two, making one piece about twice the size of the other. Shape both pieces into smooth balls. Dampen the top of the large ball and place the small ball on top. Push a lightly floured index finger through the center of the dough.

2 To make cloverleaf rolls, divide each portion of dough into three equal pieces. Shape each into a smooth ball, lightly dampen and position in a cloverleaf formation. Lightly press together.

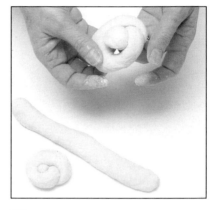

3 To make knots, roll each dough portion into a fairly long cylinder shape. Carefully knot the dough cylinder, as you would a piece of string.

4 To make braids, divide each dough portion into three equal pieces. Roll each piece into an even cylinder shape. Dampen the three cylinders at one end and pinch together. Loosely braid the cylinders. Pinch the dough together at the other end, dampening lightly first.

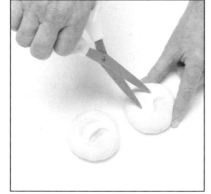

5 To make snipped-top rolls, roll each dough portion into a smooth ball. Using a pair of kitchen scissors, make two or three snips in the top of each ball.

6 To make twists, divide each dough portion into two equal pieces. Roll each piece into an even cylinder shape then twist the two pieces together, dampening at each end and pressing together firmly.

Lining Baking Pans

Ensure that your cakes and quick breads don't stick to the pan by lining the pans with waxed or parchment paper.

LINING A ROUND PAN

1 To line a round pan, place the pan on waxed or parchment paper, and draw around the edge. Cut out two rounds that size, then cut a strip, a little longer than the pan's circumference and one and a half times its depth. Lightly grease the pan, and place one paper round on the base. Make small diagonal cuts along one of the long edges of the paper strip.

2 Put the paper strip inside the pan, with the snipped fringe along the base. Place the second paper circle in the base of the pan, covering the fringe. Grease once more.

LINING A JELLY ROLL PAN

1 To line a jelly roll pan, cut a piece of waxed or parchment paper large enough to line the base and sides of the pan. Lay the paper over the pan and make four diagonal cuts, one from each corner of the paper to the nearest corner of the pan.

2 Lightly grease the pan. Place the paper in the pan and smooth into the sides, overlapping the paper corners to fit neatly.

LINING A LOAF PAN

1 To line a loaf pan, cut a strip of waxed or parchment paper three times as long as the depth of the pan and as wide as the length of the base.

2 Lightly grease the pan. Place the strip of paper in the pan so that the paper covers the base and comes up over both long sides.

Testing Cakes

It is very important to check that cakes and pastries are properly cooked, otherwise they can be soggy and cakes may sink in the middle.

TESTING A FRUITCAKE

1 To test if a fruitcake is ready, push a skewer or cake tester into it. If it comes out clean, the cake is cooked.

2 Fruit cakes are generally left to cool in the pan for 30 minutes. Then turn the cake out carefully, peel away the paper, and place on a wire rack or board.

TESTING A SPONGECAKE

1 To test if a spongecake is ready, press down lightly in the center of the cake with your fingertips – if the cake springs back, it is cooked.

2 To remove the cooked spongecake from the pan, loosen around the edge by carefully scraping around the inside of the pan with a metal spatula. Invert the cake onto a wire rack, cover with a second rack, then invert again. Remove the top rack, and let cool.

TESTING BREAD

1 To test if a loaf of bread is ready, first loosen the edges of the loaf with a metal spatula, then turn out the loaf.

2 Hold the loaf upside-down and tap it gently on the base. If it sounds hollow, the bread is cooked.

Making a Piping Bag

Being able to make your own piping bag is a very handy skill, particularly if you are dealing with small amounts of icing or several colors.

Icing a Cake

Confident icing of a cake makes all the difference in its appearance. With just a little practice, you'll have completely professional-looking cakes!

 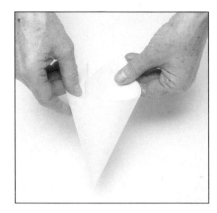 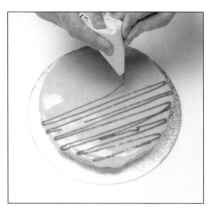 

1 Fold a 10 in square of waxed paper in half to form a triangle. Using the center of the long side as the central tip, roll half the paper into a cone.

2 Holding the paper in position, continue to roll the other half of the triangle around the first, to form a complete cone.

1 To create a simple zig-zag effect, ice the cake all over, then pipe lines in a different color backward and forward over the top.

2 To create a feathered effect, follow step 1, then drag a knife through the icing at regular intervals in opposite directions, perpendicular to the lines.

3 To make a figure of eight, or a similar effect, ice the cake all over, then, using a different colored icing, pipe figure eights around the edge of the cake, in a steady stream.

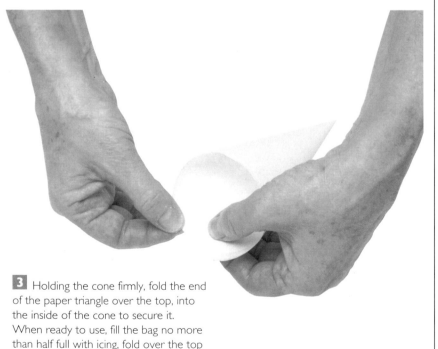 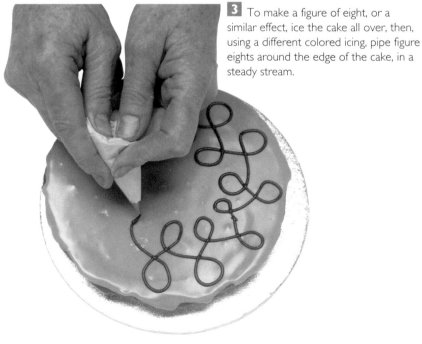

3 Holding the cone firmly, fold the end of the paper triangle over the top, into the inside of the cone to secure it. When ready to use, fill the bag no more than half full with icing, fold over the top several times to seal, then snip off the tip of the bag to the required size.

Citrus Fruits

Oranges, lemons and other citrus fruits are widely used in baking, both as flavoring and decoration.

1 To grate the rind from a citrus fruit, use the finest side of a grater. Don't remove any of the white pith, and brush off any rind which remains in the grater.

2 To pare the rind from a citrus fruit, use a swivel vegetable peeler. Remove the rind in strips as if peeling a potato, and don't remove any of the white pith.

3 To make citrus rind shreds, or juliennes, cut strips of pared rind into very fine shreds using a sharp knife. Boil the shreds for a couple of minutes in water or sugar syrup to soften them.

Making Apricot Glaze

Apricot glaze is extremely useful for brushing over any kind of fresh fruit topping or filling to give it a lovely shiny appearance.

1 Place a few spoonfuls of apricot jam in a small saucepan along with a squeeze of lemon juice. Heat the jam, stirring until it is melted and runny.

2 Pour the melted jam into a wire strainer placed over a bowl. Stir the jam with a wooden spoon to help push it right through.

3 Return the strained jam from the bowl to the pan. Keep the glaze warm, and brush it generously over the fresh fruit until evenly coated.

Banana Gingerbread Slices

Bananas make this spicy bread delightfully moist. The flavor develops on keeping, so wrap the gingerbread and store it for a few days before slicing, if possible.

Makes 20 slices

INGREDIENTS
2½ cups all-purpose flour
1 tsp baking soda
4 tsp ground ginger
2 tsp pumpkin pie spice
⅔ cup light brown sugar
4 tbsp sunflower oil
2 tbsp molasses
2 tbsp malt extract
2 large eggs
4 tbsp orange juice
3 ripe bananas
⅔ cup raisins or golden raisins

1 Preheat the oven to 350°F. Lightly grease and line an 11 x 7 in shallow baking pan with parchment paper.

2 Sift together the flour, baking soda and spices into a mixing bowl. Place the sugar in the sifter over the bowl, add some of the flour mixture and rub through the sifter with a wooden spoon.

3 Make a well in the center of the dry ingredients, and add the oil, molasses, malt extract, eggs and orange juice. Mix together thoroughly.

orange juice

malt extract   *raisins*

flour

pumpkin pie spice

light brown sugar

eggs

sunflower oil

baking soda

ground ginger   *bananas*   *molasses*

5 Scrape the mixture into the prepared baking pan. Bake for about 35–40 minutes, or until the center of the gingerbread springs back when lightly pressed.

4 Mash the bananas on a plate. Add the raisins or golden raisins to the mixture, then mix in the mashed bananas.

6 Let the gingerbread cool in the pan for 5 minutes, then turn it out onto a wire rack to cool completely. Transfer to a board, and cut into 20 slices to serve.

NUTRITIONAL NOTES
PER PORTION:

CALORIES 148
FAT 3.07 g **SATURATED FAT** 0.53 g
CHOLESTEROL 19.30 mg **FIBER** 0.79 g

COOK'S TIP
If your brown sugar is lumpy, mix it with a little flour and it will be easier to sift.

Lemon Sponge Fingers

These sponge fingers are perfect for serving with fruit salads or light, creamy desserts.

Makes about 20

INGREDIENTS
2 eggs
6 tbsp superfine sugar
grated rind of 1 lemon
½ cup all-purpose flour, sifted
superfine sugar, for sprinkling

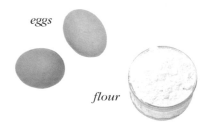

eggs

flour

superfine sugar

lemon

VARIATION

To make Spicy Orange Fingers, substitute grated orange rind for the lemon rind and add 1 tsp ground cinnamon with the flour.

NUTRITIONAL NOTES

PER PORTION:

CALORIES 33
FAT 0.57 g **SATURATED FAT** 0.16 g
CHOLESTEROL 19.30 mg **FIBER** 0.08 g

1 Preheat the oven to 375°F. Line two baking sheets with parchment paper. Whisk the eggs, sugar and lemon rind together with a hand-held electric mixer until thick and like a mousse (when the whisk is lifted, a trail should remain on the surface of the mixture for at least 15 seconds). Gently fold in the all-purpose flour with a large, metal spoon, using a figure eight action.

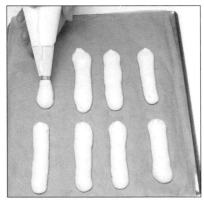

2 Place the mixture in a large pastry bag fitted with a ½ in plain tip. Pipe the mixture into finger lengths onto the prepared baking sheets.

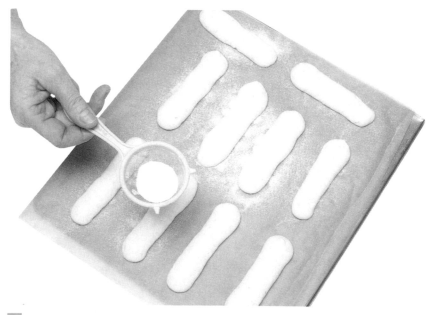

3 Sprinkle the fingers with superfine sugar. Bake for 6–8 minutes until golden brown, then transfer the sponge fingers to a wire rack to cool.

Snowballs

These light, almost fat-free morsels make an excellent accompaniment to yogurt ice cream.

Makes about 20

INGREDIENTS
2 large egg whites
$\frac{1}{2}$ cup superfine sugar
1 tbsp cornstarch, sifted
1 tsp white wine vinegar
$1\frac{1}{4}$ tsp vanilla extract

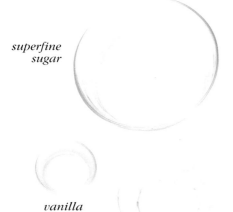

superfine sugar

vanilla extract

cornstarch

eggs

white wine vinegar

1 Preheat the oven to 300°F, and line two baking sheets with parchment paper. Using a hand-held electric mixer, beat the egg whites in a very clean bowl until stiff peaks form.

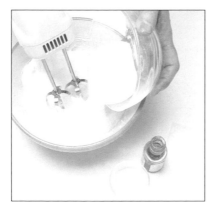

2 Add the superfine sugar, a little at a time, beating until the meringue is very stiff. Beat in the cornstarch, vinegar and vanilla extract.

NUTRITIONAL NOTES
Per portion:
CALORIES 29
FAT 0.01 g **SATURATED FAT** 0
CHOLESTEROL 0 **FIBER** 0

VARIATION

Make Pineapple Snowballs by folding about $\frac{1}{4}$ cup finely chopped semi-dried pineapple into the meringue mixture.

3 Using a teaspoon, mound the mixture into balls on the prepared baking sheets. Bake for 30 minutes.

4 Cool slightly on the baking sheets, then transfer the snowballs to a wire rack to cool completely.

Filo and Apricot Purses

Filo pastry is very easy to use and is low in fat. Keep a package on hand in the freezer, so you're always ready to whip up an afternoon snack.

Makes 12

INGREDIENTS
¾ cup dried apricots
3 tbsp apricot jam
3 amaretti cookies, crushed
3 filo pastry sheets
4 tsp margarine, melted
confectioner's sugar, for dusting

filo pastry

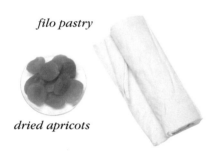

dried apricots

apricot jam

margarine

*amaretti
cookies*

COOK'S TIP

The easiest way to crush amaretti cookies, is to put them in a plastic bag and roll them with a rolling pin.

NUTRITIONAL NOTES

PER PORTION:

CALORIES 58
FAT 1.85 g **SATURATED FAT** 0.40 g
CHOLESTEROL 0.12 mg **FIBER** 0.74 g

1 Preheat the oven to 350°F. Grease two baking sheets. Chop the apricots, put them in a bowl, and stir in the apricot jam. Add the crushed amaretti cookies, and mix well.

2 Cut the filo pastry into twenty-four 5 in squares, pile the squares on top of each other, and cover with a clean dish towel to prevent the pastry from drying out and becoming brittle.

3 Lay one pastry square onto a flat surface, brush lightly with melted margarine, and lay another square diagonally on top. Brush the top square with melted margarine. Spoon a small mound of apricot mixture in the center of the pastry, bring up the edges, and pinch together in a money-bag shape. Repeat with the remaining filo squares and filling to make twelve purses in all.

4 Arrange the purses on the prepared baking sheets, and bake for 5–8 minutes until golden brown. Transfer to a wire rack, and dust lightly with confectioner's sugar. Serve warm.

Filo Scrunchies

Quick and easy to make, these pastries make an ideal afternoon snack. Eat them warm, or they will lose their crispness.

Makes 6

INGREDIENTS
5 apricots or plums
4 filo pastry sheets
4 tsp margarine, melted
1/3 cup raw sugar
2 tbsp sliced almonds
confectioner's sugar, for dusting

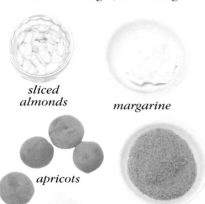

sliced almonds

margarine

apricots

raw sugar

filo pastry

COOK'S TIP

Filo pastry dries out very quickly. Keep it covered as much as possible with a dry cloth or plastic wrap to limit exposure to the air, or it will become too brittle to use.

NUTRITIONAL NOTES
PER PORTION:

CALORIES 132
FAT 4.19 g **SATURATED FAT** 0.63 g
CHOLESTEROL 0 **FIBER** 0.67 g

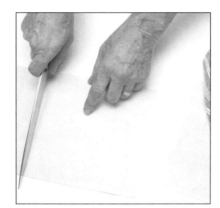

1 Preheat the oven to 375°F. Halve the apricots or plums, remove the pits, and slice the fruit. Cut the filo pastry into twelve 7 in squares. Pile the squares on top of each other, and cover with a clean dish towel to prevent the pastry from drying out.

2 Remove one square of filo and brush it with melted margarine. Lay a second filo square on top, then, using your fingers, mold the pastry into folds. Make five more scrunchies in the same way, working quickly so that the pastry does not dry out.

3 Arrange a few slices of fruit in the folds of each scrunchie, then sprinkle generously with the raw sugar and sliced almonds. Place the scrunchies on a baking sheet.

4 Bake the scrunchies for about 8–10 minutes until golden brown, then loosen them from the baking sheet with a metal spatula, and transfer them to a wire rack. Dust with confectioner's sugar and serve at once.

Banana and Apricot Chelsea Buns

Old favorites are given a low fat twist with a delectable fruit filling.

Makes 9

INGREDIENTS
6 tbsp warm skim milk
1 tsp dried yeast
pinch of sugar
2 cups white bread flour
2 tsp pumpkin pie spice
1/2 tsp salt
2 tbsp margarine
1/4 cup sugar
1 large egg, lightly beaten

FOR THE FILLING
1 large ripe banana
1 cup dried apricots
2 tbsp light brown sugar

FOR THE GLAZE
2 tbsp sugar
2 tbsp water

dried yeast

egg

dried apricots

margarine

brown sugar

banana

pumpkin pie spice

sugar

white bread flour

salt

skim milk

1 Grease a 7 in square cake pan. Put the warm milk in a small pitcher. Sprinkle the yeast on top. Add a pinch of sugar to help activate the yeast, mix well, and let stand for 30 minutes.

2 Sift the flour, spice and salt into a mixing bowl. Work in the margarine, then stir in the sugar. Make a well in the center, then pour in the yeast mixture and the egg. Gradually stir in the flour to make a soft dough. Add milk if needed.

3 Turn the dough out onto a floured surface and knead for 5 minutes until smooth and elastic. Return to the clean bowl, cover with a damp dish towel, and let rise in a warm place or about 2 hours, or until doubled in bulk.

4 Meanwhile prepare the filling. Mash the banana in a bowl. Using kitchen scissors, cut up the apricots and add to the mashed banana with the sugar.

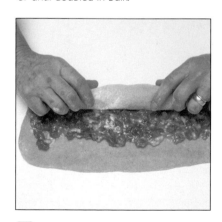

5 Knead the risen dough on a floured surface for 2 minutes, then roll out to a 12 x 9 in rectangle. Spread the banana and apricot filling over the dough, and roll up lengthwise like a jelly roll, with the join underneath.

NUTRITIONAL NOTES

Per portion:

CALORIES 214
FAT 3.18 g **SATURATED FAT** 0.63 g
CHOLESTEROL 21.59 mg **FIBER** 2.18 g

6 Cut the roll into nine pieces and place, cut-side down, in the prepared pan. Cover and let rise in a warm place for about 30 minutes. Preheat the oven to 400°F.

7 Bake the buns for 20–25 minutes until golden brown and cooked in the center. Meanwhile make the glaze. Mix the sugar and water in a small saucepan. Heat, stirring, until dissolved, then boil for 2 minutes. Brush the glaze over the buns while still hot, then remove the buns from the pan and let cool on a wire rack.

Raspberry Muffins

These muffins are made with baking powder and low fat buttermilk, giving them a light and spongy texture. They are delicious at any time of the day.

Makes 10–12

INGREDIENTS
2½ cups all-purpose flour
1 tbsp baking powder
½ cup sugar
1 large egg
1 cup buttermilk
4 tbsp sunflower oil
1 cup raspberries

egg

buttermilk

sunflower oil

sugar

flour

baking powder

raspberries

1 Preheat the oven to 400°F. Arrange twelve cupcake holders in a deep muffin pan. Sift the flour and baking powder into a mixing bowl, stir in the sugar, then make a well in the center.

2 Stir the egg, buttermilk and sunflower oil together in a bowl, pour into the flour mixture, and stir quickly until just combined.

3 Add the raspberries, and lightly fold them in with a metal spoon. Spoon the mixture into the cupcake holders, filling them two-thirds full.

4 Bake the muffins for 20–25 minutes until golden brown and firm in the middle. Transfer to a wire rack, and serve warm or cold.

Date and Apple Muffins

You'll only need one or two of these wholesome muffins per person, since they are very filling.

Makes 12

INGREDIENTS

1¼ cups self-rising whole-wheat flour
1¼ cups self-rising white flour
1 tsp ground cinnamon
1 tsp baking powder
2 tbsp margarine
½ cup light brown sugar
1 eating apple
1 cup apple juice
2 tbsp pear and apple spread
1 large egg, lightly beaten
½ cup chopped dates
1 tbsp chopped pecan halves

chopped dates

egg

pecans

self-rising whole-wheat flour

ground cinnamon

light brown sugar

self-rising white flour

apple juice

margarine

pear and apple spread

eating apple

baking powder

1 Preheat the oven to 400°F. Arrange twelve cupcake holders in a deep muffin pan. Put the whole-wheat flour in a mixing bowl. Sift in the white flour with the cinnamon and baking powder. Work in the margarine until the mixture resembles bread crumbs, then stir in the light brown sugar.

2 Quarter and core the apple, finely chop it, and set aside. Stir a little of the apple juice with the pear and apple spread until smooth. Stir in the remaining juice, then add to the flour mixture with the egg. Add the chopped apple to the bowl with the dates. Stir quickly until just combined.

3 Divide the batter evenly among the cupcake holders.

4 Sprinkle the muffins with the chopped pecan halves. Bake for about 20–25 minutes until golden brown and firm in the middle. Remove to a wire rack, and serve while still warm.

NUTRITIONAL NOTES

PER PORTION:

CALORIES 163
FAT 2.98 g **SATURATED FAT** 0.47 g
CHOLESTEROL 16.04 mg **FIBER** 1.97 g

Brown Sugar Meringues

These light brown meringues are extremely low in fat and are delicious served on their own, or sandwiched together with a fresh fruit and soft cheese filling.

Makes about 20

INGREDIENTS
²/₃ cup light brown sugar
2 large egg whites
1 tsp finely chopped walnuts

eggs

light brown sugar

walnuts

NUTRITIONAL NOTES
PER PORTION:

CALORIES 30
FAT 0.34 g **SATURATED FAT** 0.04 g
CHOLESTEROL 0 **FIBER** 0.02 g

COOK'S TIP

For a sophisticated filling, mix ½ cup nonfat cream cheese with 1 tbsp confectioner's sugar. Chop 2 slices of fresh pineapple, and add to the mixture. Use to sandwich the meringues together in pairs.

1 Preheat the oven to 325°F. Line two baking sheets with parchment paper. Press the sugar through a metal strainer into a bowl.

2 Whisk the egg whites in a clean bowl until very stiff and dry, then whisk in the sugar, about 1 tbsp at a time, until the meringue is very thick and glossy.

3 Spoon small mounds of the mixture onto the prepared baking sheets.

4 Sprinkle the meringues with the chopped walnuts. Bake for 30 minutes. Cool for 5 minutes on the baking sheets, then let cool on a wire rack.

Apricot and Almond Fingers

These almond fingers will stay moist for several days, thanks to the addition of apricots.

Makes 18

INGREDIENTS
2 cups self-rising flour
²/₃ cup light brown sugar
¹/₃ cup semolina
1 cup dried apricots, chopped
2 large eggs
2 tbsp malt extract
2 tbsp honey
4 tbsp skim milk
4 tbsp sunflower oil
few drops of almond extract
2 tbsp sliced almonds

1 Preheat the oven to 325°F. Lightly grease and line an 11 x 7 in shallow baking pan. Sift the flour into a bowl, and add the brown sugar, semolina, chopped dried apricots and eggs. Add the malt extract, honey, milk, sunflower oil and almond extract. Mix well until the mixture is smooth.

honey

skim milk

sunflower oil

eggs

dried apricots

light brown sugar

semolina

self-rising flour

malt extract

sliced almonds

2 Turn the mixture into the prepared pan, spread to the edges, and sprinkle with the sliced almonds.

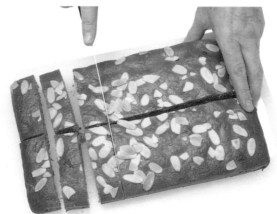

3 Bake for 30–35 minutes, or until the center of the cake springs back when lightly pressed. Transfer to a wire rack to cool. Remove the paper, place the cake on a board, and cut it into eighteen slices with a sharp knife.

NUTRITIONAL NOTES
PER PORTION:

CALORIES 153
FAT 4.56 g **SATURATED FAT** 0.61 g
CHOLESTEROL 21.50 mg **FIBER** 1.27 g

Coffee Sponge Drops

These are delicious on their own, but taste even better with a filling of nonfat cream cheese and drained and chopped preserved ginger.

Makes 12

INGREDIENTS
1/2 cup all-purpose flour
1 tbsp instant coffee powder
2 large eggs
6 tbsp superfine sugar

FOR THE FILLING
1/2 cup nonfat cream cheese
1/4 cup chopped preserved ginger

instant coffee powder

eggs

flour

superfine sugar

nonfat cream cheese

preserved ginger

NUTRITIONAL NOTES

PER PORTION:

CALORIES 69
FAT 1.36 g **SATURATED FAT** 0.50 g
CHOLESTEROL 33.33 mg **FIBER** 0.29 g

1 Preheat the oven to 375°F. Line two baking sheets with parchment paper. Make the filling by beating together the cheese and ginger. Refrigerate until ready to use. Sift the flour and instant coffee powder together.

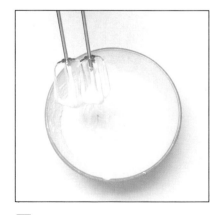

2 Combine the eggs and superfine sugar in a bowl. Beat with a hand-held electric mixer until thick and like a mousse (when the mixer is lifted, a trail should remain on the surface of the mixture for at least 15 seconds).

3 Gently fold in the sifted flour and coffee mixture with a metal spoon, taking care not to knock out any air.

4 Spoon the mixture into a pastry bag fitted with a 1/2 in plain tip. Pipe 1 1/2 in rounds onto the baking sheets. Bake for 12 minutes. Cool on a wire rack, then sandwich together with the filling.

Oaty Crisps

These cookies are very crisp and crunchy – ideal to serve with morning coffee.

Makes 18

INGREDIENTS
1¾ cups rolled oats
½ cup light brown sugar
1 large egg
4 tbsp sunflower oil
2 tbsp malt extract

malt extract   *sunflower oil*

rolled oats

light brown sugar   *egg*

NUTRITIONAL NOTES
PER PORTION:

CALORIES 86
FAT 3.59 g **SATURATED FAT** 0.57 g
CHOLESTEROL 10.70 mg **FIBER** 0.66 g

VARIATION
To give these crisp cookies a coarser texture, substitute jumbo oats for some or all of the rolled oats.

1 Preheat the oven to 375°F. Lightly grease two baking sheets. Combine the rolled oats and brown sugar in a bowl, breaking up any lumps in the sugar. Add the egg, sunflower oil and malt extract, mix together well, then let soak for about 15 minutes.

2 Using a teaspoon, place small mounds of the mixture well apart on the prepared baking sheets. Press the mounds into 3 in rounds with the back of a dampened fork.

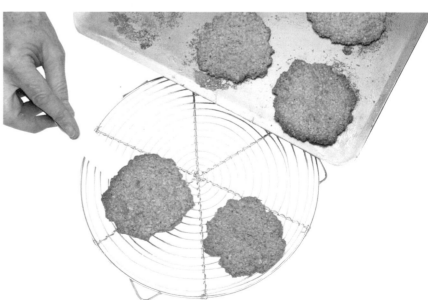

3 Bake the cookies for 10–15 minutes until golden brown. Let cool for 1 minute, then remove with a metal spatula, and cool on a wire rack.

Irish Whiskey Cake

This moist, rich fruitcake is drizzled with whiskey as soon as it comes out of the oven.

Serves 12

INGREDIENTS
²/₃ cup candied cherries
1 cup dark brown sugar
²/₃ cup golden raisins
²/₃ cup raisins
½ cup currants
1¼ cups cold tea
2½ cups self-rising flour, sifted
1 large egg
3 tbsp Irish whiskey

raisins

currants

golden raisins

brown sugar

candied cherries

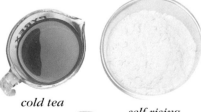

cold tea

Irish whiskey

self-rising flour

egg

COOK'S TIP
If time is short, use hot tea and soak the fruit for just 2 hours.

1 Mix the cherries, sugar, dried fruit and tea in a large bowl. Soak overnight, until all the tea has been absorbed into the fruit.

2 Preheat the oven to 350°F. Grease and line a 9 x 4 in loaf pan. Add the flour, then the egg to the fruit mixture, and beat thoroughly until well combined.

NUTRITIONAL NOTES
PER PORTION:

CALORIES 265
FAT 0.88 g **SATURATED FAT** 0.25 g
CHOLESTEROL 16.00 mg **FIBER** 1.48 g

3 Pour the mixture into the prepared pan, and bake for 1½ hours, or until a skewer inserted into the center of the cake comes out clean.

4 While the cake is still hot, prick the top with a skewer, and drizzle with the whiskey. Allow to stand for about 5 minutes; then remove from the pan, and cool on a wire rack.

Fruit and Nut Cake

A rich fruitcake that improves with keeping.

Serves 12–14

INGREDIENTS

1½ cups self-rising whole-
  wheat flour
1½ cups self-rising white flour
2 tsp pumpkin pie spice
1 tbsp apple and apricot spread
3 tbsp honey
1 tbsp molasses
6 tbsp sunflower oil
¾ cup orange juice
2 large eggs, beaten
4 cups mixed dried fruit
3 tbsp almond halves
½ cup candied cherries, halved

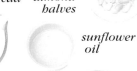

mixed dried fruit

molasses

honey pumpkin pie spice

eggs

apple and apricot spread

orange juice

almond halves

sunflower oil

self-rising white flour

candied cherries

self-rising whole-wheat flour

1 Preheat the oven to 325°F. Grease and line a deep, round 8 in cake pan. Secure a band of brown paper around the outside.

2 Sift the flours into a mixing bowl with the pumpkin pie spice, and make a well in the center.

NUTRITIONAL NOTES

PER PORTION:

CALORIES 333
FAT 8.54 g **SATURATED FAT** 1.12 g
CHOLESTEROL 29.62 mg **FIBER** 3.08 g

3 Put the apple and apricot spread in a small bowl. Gradually stir in the honey and molasses. Add to the dry ingredients with the oil, orange juice, eggs and dried fruit. Mix thoroughly.

4 Pour the batter into the prepared pan, and smooth the surface. Arrange the almonds and cherries over the top. Place the pan on newspaper, and bake for about 2 hours, or until a skewer inserted into the center comes out clean. Transfer to a wire rack until cold, then turn out of the pan, and remove the paper.

Chocolate Banana Cake

A chocolate cake that's deliciously low in fat – it is moist enough to eat without icing if you want to cut down on calories.

NUTRITIONAL NOTES
PER PORTION:

CALORIES 411
FAT 8.79 g **SATURATED FAT** 2.06 g
CHOLESTEROL 48.27 mg **FIBER** 2.06 g

Serves 8

INGREDIENTS
2 cups self-rising flour
3 tbsp reduced-fat cocoa powder
²/₃ cup light brown sugar
2 tbsp malt extract
2 tbsp corn syrup
2 large eggs
¼ cup skim milk
2 large, ripe bananas
4 tbsp sunflower oil

FOR THE ICINGS
2 cups confectioner's sugar, sifted
7 tsp reduced-fat cocoa powder, sifted
1–2 tbsp warm water

corn syrup
eggs
skim milk
confectioner's sugar
self-rising flour
reduced-fat cocoa powder
sunflower oil
bananas
malt extract
light brown sugar

1 Preheat the oven to 325°F. Grease and line a deep, round 8 in cake pan.

2 Sift the flour into a mixing bowl with the cocoa powder. Stir in the sugar.

3 Make a well in the center, and add the malt extract, corn syrup, eggs, milk and oil. Mash the bananas thoroughly, and stir them into the mixture until thoroughly combined.

4 Pour the cake mixture into the prepared pan, and bake for 1–1¼ hours, or until the center of the cake springs back when lightly pressed.

5 Remove the cake from the pan, and let cool on a wire rack.

COOK'S TIP
This cake also makes a delicious dessert if heated in the microwave. The icing melts to a puddle of sauce. Serve a slice topped with a large dollop of low fat ricotta cheese for a really special treat.

6 Reserve ½ cup confectioner's sugar and 1 tsp cocoa powder. Make a darker icing by beating the remaining sugar and cocoa powder with enough of the warm water to make a thick icing. Pour it over the top of the cake, and spread evenly to the edges. Make a thinner, lighter icing by mixing the remaining confectioner's sugar and cocoa powder with a few drops of water. Drizzle or pipe this icing across the top of the cake to decorate.

Mango and Amaretti Strudel

Fresh mango and crushed amaretti wrapped in wafer-thin filo pastry make a special treat that is just as delicious made with apricots or plums.

Serves 4

INGREDIENTS
1 large mango
grated rind of 1 lemon
2 amaretti cookies
3 tbsp raw sugar
4 tbsp whole-wheat bread crumbs
2 sheets filo pastry, each 19 x 11 in
4 tsp margarine, melted
1 tbsp chopped almonds
confectioner's sugar, for dusting

NUTRITIONAL NOTES

PER PORTION:

CALORIES 239
FAT 8.45 g **SATURATED FAT** 4.43 g
CHOLESTEROL 17.25 mg **FIBER** 3.30 g

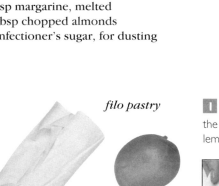

filo pastry

mango

whole-wheat breadcrumbs

lemon rind

raw sugar

amaretti cookies

soft margarine

chopped almonds

1 Preheat the oven to 375°F. Lightly grease a large baking sheet. Halve, pit and peel the mango. Cut into cubes, then place them in a bowl, and sprinkle with the grated lemon rind.

2 Crush the amaretti cookies, and mix them with the raw sugar and the whole-wheat bread crumbs.

3 Lay one sheet of filo on a flat surface, and brush with a quarter of the melted margarine. Top with the second sheet, brush with one-third of the remaining margarine, then fold both sheets over, to make a rectangle measuring 11 x 9½ in. Brush with half the remaining margarine.

4 Sprinkle the filo with the amaretti mixture, leaving a 2 in border on each long side. Arrange the mango cubes over the top.

5 Roll up the filo from one of the long sides, jelly roll fashion. Lift the strudel onto the baking sheet with the join underneath. Brush with the remaining melted margarine, and sprinkle with the chopped almonds.

6 Bake for 20–25 minutes until golden brown, then transfer to a board. Dust with confectioner's sugar, slice diagonally, and serve warm.

COOK'S TIP
The easiest way to prepare a mango is to cut horizontally through the fruit, keeping the knife blade close to the pit. Repeat on the other side of the pit, and peel off the skin. Remove the remaining skin and flesh from around the pit.

Angel Food Cake

Serve this light-as-air cake with low fat ricotta
cheese – it makes a delicious dessert.

Serves 10

INGREDIENTS
¹/₃ cup all-purpose flour
¹/₃ cup cornstarch
8 large egg whites
1 cup superfine sugar, plus
    extra for sprinkling
1 tsp vanilla extract
confectioner's sugar, for dusting

cornstarch

vanilla extract

flour

superfine
sugar

eggs

1 Preheat the oven to 350°F. Sift the
flour and cornstarch together onto a
sheet of waxed paper.

2 Whisk the egg whites in a large,
clean bowl until very stiff, then gradually
add the sugar and vanilla extract,
whisking until the mixture becomes thick
and glossy.

COOK'S TIP

Make a lemony icing by mixing
1¹/₂ cups confectioner's sugar with
1–2 tbsp lemon juice. Drizzle the
icing over the cake, and decorate
with physalis or lemon slices and
mint sprigs.

3 Gently fold in the flour mixture with
a large, metal spoon. Spoon into an
ungreased 10 in angel food cake pan,
smooth the surface, and bake for about
45–50 minutes, until the cake springs
back when lightly pressed.

4 Sprinkle a piece of waxed paper
with superfine sugar, and place an egg
cup in the center. Invert the cake pan
and balance it carefully on the egg cup.
When cold, the cake will drop out of the
pan. Transfer it to a plate, ice if desired
(see Cook's Tip), then dust with
confectioner's sugar and serve.

Pear Quick Bread

This is an ideal quick bread to make when pears are plentiful – an excellent use for windfalls.

Serves 6–8

INGREDIENTS
scant ¹/₃ cup rolled oats
¹/₃ cup light brown sugar
2 tbsp pear or apple juice
2 tbsp sunflower oil
2 small pears
1 cup self-rising flour
²/₃ cup golden raisins
¹/₂ tsp baking powder
2 tsp pumpkin pie spice
1 egg

small pears
egg
baking powder
sunflower oil

self-rising flour

rolled oats
golden raisins

pumpkin pie spice

light brown sugar
pear juice

NUTRITIONAL NOTES
PER PORTION:

CALORIES 200
FAT 4.61 g **SATURATED FAT** 0.79 g
CHOLESTEROL 27.50 mg **FIBER** 1.39 g

1 Preheat the oven to 350°F. Grease and line a 9 × 3¹/₂ in loaf pan with parchment paper. Put the oats in a bowl with the sugar, pear or apple juice and oil, mix well, and let stand for 15 minutes.

2 Quarter, core and grate the pears. Add to the oat mixture with the flour, golden raisins, baking powder, pumpkin pie spice and egg. Stir together until thoroughly combined.

3 Spoon the mixture into the prepared loaf pan, and level the top. Bake for 50–60 minutes, or until a skewer inserted into the center comes out clean.

4 Transfer the quick bread onto a wire rack, and peel off the parchment paper. Let cool completely.

COOK'S TIP
Health food stores sell concentrated pear and apple juice, ready for diluting as required.

Peach Jelly Roll

A feather-light sponge enclosing peach jam –
delicious at tea time.

Serves 6–8

INGREDIENTS
3 large eggs
$\frac{1}{2}$ cup superfine sugar
$\frac{3}{4}$ cup all-purpose flour, sifted
1 tbsp boiling water
6 tbsp peach jam
confectioner's sugar, for dusting
    (optional)

eggs

flour

*superfine
sugar*

peach jam

NUTRITIONAL NOTES

PER PORTION:

CALORIES 178
FAT 2.45 g **SATURATED FAT** 0.67 g
CHOLESTEROL 82.50 mg **FIBER** 0.33 g

COOK'S TIP

Decorate the jelly roll with a quick
white icing. Put 4 oz icing in a pastry
bag fitted with a small writing tip,
and pipe lines over the top of the
jelly roll.

1 Preheat the oven to 400°F. Lightly
grease a 12 x 8 in jelly roll tin, and line
with parchment paper. Combine the
eggs and sugar in a large bowl and
beat together with a hand-held electric
mixer until thick and like a mousse
(when the whisk is lifted, a trail should
remain on the surface of the mixture for
at least 15 seconds).

2 Carefully fold in the flour with a
large, metal spoon, then add the boiling
water in the same way.

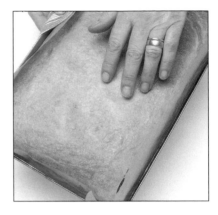

3 Spoon into the prepared pan, spread
evenly to the edges, and bake for about
10–12 minutes, until the cake springs
back when lightly pressed.

4 Spread a sheet of waxed paper on a
flat surface, sprinkle it with superfine
sugar, then invert the cake onto it. Peel
off the parchment paper.

5 Neatly trim the edges of the cake.
Make a neat cut two-thirds of the way
through the cake, about $\frac{1}{2}$ in from the
short edge nearest you.

6 Spread the cake with the peach jam,
and roll up quickly from the partially cut
end. Hold in position for a minute,
making sure the seam is underneath.
Cool on a wire rack. Decorate with icing
(see Cook's Tip) or simply dust with
confectioner's sugar before serving.

Banana and Ginger Quick Bread

Serve this quick bread with a low fat spread. The preserved ginger adds an interesting flavor.

Serves 6–8

INGREDIENTS
1½ cups self-rising flour
1 tsp baking powder
3 tbsp margarine
⅓ cup dark brown sugar
⅓ cup drained preserved
  ginger, chopped
4 tbsp skim milk
2 ripe bananas, mashed

baking powder

preserved ginger

dark brown sugar

bananas

self-rising flour

skim milk

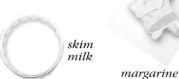
margarine

1 Preheat the oven to 350°F. Grease and line a 9 × 3½ in loaf pan. Sift the flour and baking powder into a bowl.

2 Work in the margarine until the mixture resembles bread crumbs.

VARIATION
To make Banana and Golden Raisin Quick Bread, add 1 tsp pumpkin pie spice and omit the ginger. Stir in ⅔ cup golden raisins.

3 Stir in the sugar. Add the ginger, milk and bananas, and mix to a soft batter.

4 Spoon into the prepared pan, and bake for 40–45 minutes. Run a metal spatula around the edges to loosen the quick bread, then turn it onto a wire rack, and let cool.

Spiced Apple Cake

Grated apple and chopped dates give this cake a natural sweetness – omit 1 oz of the sugar if the fruit is very sweet.

Serves 8

INGREDIENTS

2 cups self-rising whole-wheat flour
1 tsp baking powder
2 tsp ground cinnamon
1 cup chopped dates
½ cup light brown sugar
1 tbsp pear and apple spread
½ cup apple juice
2 large eggs
6 tbsp sunflower oil
2 eating apples, cored and grated
1 tbsp chopped walnuts

apple juice

ground cinnamon

sunflower oil

self-rising whole-wheat flour

chopped walnuts

chopped dates

baking powder

light brown sugar

pear and apple spread

eating apples

eggs

1 Preheat the oven to 350°F. Grease and line a deep, round 8 in cake pan with parchment paper. Sift the flour, baking powder and cinnamon into a mixing bowl, stir in the dates, and make a well in the center.

2 Mix the sugar with the pear and apple spread in a small bowl. Gradually stir in the apple juice. Add to the dry ingredients, along with the eggs, oil and apples. Combine thoroughly.

COOK'S TIP

You do not need to peel the apples – the skin adds fiber, and it softens on cooking.

3 Spoon the mixture into the prepared cake pan, sprinkle with the walnuts, and bake for 60–65 minutes, or until a skewer inserted into the center of the cake comes out clean. Transfer to a wire rack, peel off the parchment paper, and let cool.

NUTRITIONAL NOTES

PER PORTION:

CALORIES 331
FAT 11.41 g **SATURATED FAT** 1.68 g
CHOLESTEROL 48.13 mg **FIBER** 2.50 g

Herb Triangles

Stuffed with cooked chicken and salad, these make a good lunchtime snack and are also an ideal accompaniment to a bowl of steaming soup.

Makes 8

INGREDIENTS
2 cups whole-wheat flour
1 cup white bread flour
1 tsp salt
½ tsp baking soda
1 tsp cream of tartar
½ tsp chili powder
¼ cup margarine
4 tbsp chopped mixed fresh herbs
1 cup skim milk
1 tbsp sesame seeds

mixed fresh herbs

chili powder

sesame seeds

whole-wheat flour

baking soda

cream of tartar

margarine

skim milk

salt

bread flour

1 Preheat the oven to 425°F. Lightly flour a baking sheet. Put the whole-wheat flour in a mixing bowl. Sift in the remaining dry ingredients, including the chili powder, then work in the margarine.

2 Add the herbs and milk, and mix quickly to a soft dough. Turn onto a lightly floured surface. Knead only very briefly, or the dough will become tough. Roll out to a 9 in round, and place on the prepared baking sheet. Brush lightly with water and sprinkle evenly with the sesame seeds.

3 Carefully cut the dough round into eight wedges, separate them slightly, and bake for 15–20 minutes. Transfer to a wire rack to cool. Serve warm or cold.

NUTRITIONAL NOTES
PER PORTION:

CALORIES 222
FAT 7.22 g **SATURATED FAT** 1.25 g
CHOLESTEROL 1.06 mg **FIBER** 3.54 g

VARIATION

To make Sun-dried Tomato Triangles, replace the fresh mixed herbs with 2 tbsp drained, chopped sun-dried tomatoes in oil, and add 1 tbsp each of mild paprika, chopped fresh parsley and chopped fresh marjoram.

Caraway Bread Sticks

Ideal to nibble with drinks, these can be made with all sorts of other seeds – try cumin seeds, poppy seeds or celery seeds.

Makes about 20

INGREDIENTS
²/₃ cup warm water
¹/₂ tsp dried yeast
pinch of sugar
2 cups all-purpose flour
¹/₂ tsp salt
2 tsp caraway seeds

dried yeast

caraway seeds

flour

water

salt

NUTRITIONAL NOTES

PER PORTION:

CALORIES 45
FAT 0.24 g **SATURATED FAT** 0.02 g
CHOLESTEROL 0 **FIBER** 0.39 g

VARIATION

To make Coriander and Sesame Sticks, replace the caraway seeds with 15 ml/1 tbsp crushed coriander seeds. Dampen the bread sticks lightly and sprinkle them with sesame seeds before baking.

1 Grease two baking sheets. Put the warm water in a small pitcher. Sprinkle the yeast on the top. Add the sugar, mix well, and let stand for 10 minutes.

2 Sift the flour and salt into a mixing bowl, stir in the caraway seeds, and make a well in the center. Add the yeast mixture, and gradually incorporate the flour to make a soft dough, adding a little water if necessary.

3 Turn onto a lightly floured surface, and knead for 5 minutes until smooth. Divide the mixture into twenty pieces, and roll each one into a 12 in stick. Arrange on the baking sheets, leaving room for rising, then let stand for 30 minutes until well risen. Meanwhile, preheat the oven to 425°F.

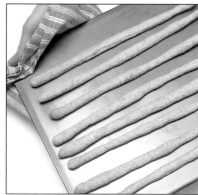

4 Bake the bread sticks for about 10–12 minutes until golden brown. Cool on the baking sheets.

Poppy Seed Rolls

Pile these soft rolls in a basket, and serve them for breakfast or with dinner.

NUTRITIONAL NOTES

PER PORTION:

CALORIES 160
FAT 2.42 g **SATURATED FAT** 0.46 g
CHOLESTEROL 32.58 mg **FIBER** 1.16 g

Makes 12

INGREDIENTS
1¼ cups warm skim milk
1 tsp dried yeast
pinch of sugar
4 cups white bread flour
1 tsp salt
1 large egg, beaten

FOR THE TOPPING
1 large egg, beaten
poppy seeds

white bread flour

skim milk

poppy seeds

egg

salt

dried yeast

1 Put half the warm milk in a small bowl. Sprinkle the yeast on the top. Add the sugar, stir well, and let stand for 30 minutes.

2 Sift the flour and salt into a mixing bowl. Make a well in the center, and pour in the yeast mixture and the egg. Gradually incorporate the flour, adding enough of the remaining milk to make a soft dough.

3 Turn the dough onto a floured surface, and knead for 5 minutes until smooth and elastic. Return to the clean bowl, cover with a damp dish towel, and let rise in a warm place for about 1 hour, or until doubled in bulk.

4 Lightly grease two baking sheets. Turn the dough onto a floured surface. Knead for 2 minutes, then cut into twelve pieces and shape into rolls.

5 Place the rolls on the prepared baking sheets, cover loosely with a large plastic bag (ballooning it to trap the air inside), and let stand in a warm place until the rolls have risen well. Preheat the oven to 425°F.

6 Brush the rolls with beaten egg, sprinkle with poppy seeds, and bake for 12–15 minutes until golden brown. Transfer to a wire rack to cool.

COOK'S TIP

Use rapid-rise dried yeast if you prefer. Add it directly to the dry ingredients and mix with lukewarm milk. The rolls will only require one rising (see package instructions). Vary the toppings. Linseed, sesame seeds and caraway seeds are all good. For extra flavor, try adding caraway seeds to the dough.

Chive and Potato Biscuits

These little treats should be fairly thin, soft and crisp on the outside. Serve them for breakfast.

Makes 20

INGREDIENTS
1 lb potatoes, peeled
1 cup all-purpose flour, sifted
2 tbsp olive oil
2 tbsp snipped chives
salt and freshly ground black pepper
low fat spread, for topping
   (optional)

potatoes

black pepper

olive oil

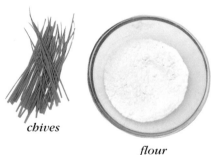
chives

flour

salt

NUTRITIONAL NOTES
PER PORTION:
CALORIES 50
FAT 1.24 g **SATURATED FAT** 0.17 g
CHOLESTEROL 0 **FIBER** 0.54 g

1 Cook the potatoes in a saucepan of boiling, salted water for 20 minutes or until tender, then drain thoroughly. Return the potatoes to the clean pan and mash them. Preheat a griddle or heavy-bottomed frying pan.

2 Add the flour, olive oil and snipped chives with a little salt and pepper to the hot mashed potato in the pan. Mix until a soft dough is formed.

COOK'S TIP

Cook the biscuits over low heat so that the outsides do not burn before the insides are cooked through.

3 Roll out the dough on a well-floured surface to a thickness of $^1/_4$ in, and stamp out rounds with a 2 in plain pastry cutter. Lightly grease the griddle or pan.

4 Cook the biscuits, in batches, on the hot griddle or frying pan for about 10 minutes, turning once, until they are golden brown on both sides. Keep the heat low. Top with a little low fat spread, if you like, and serve immediately.

Ham and Tomato Biscuits

These make an ideal accompaniment for soup. Choose a strongly flavored ham, and chop it fairly finely, so that a little goes a long way.

Makes 12

INGREDIENTS

2 cups self-rising flour
1 tsp dry mustard
1 tsp paprika, plus extra for
   sprinkling
1/2 tsp salt
2 tbsp margarine
1 tbsp snipped fresh basil
1/3 cup drained, oil packed sun-dried
   tomatoes, chopped
2 oz Black Forest ham, chopped
1/2–2/3 cup skim milk, plus extra
   for brushing

margarine

paprika

salt

skim milk

self-rising flour

fresh basil

dry mustard

sun-dried tomatoes

Black Forest ham

1 Preheat the oven to 400°F. Flour a large baking sheet. Sift together the flour, mustard, paprika and salt into a bowl. Work in the margarine until the mixture resembles bread crumbs.

2 Stir in the basil, sun-dried tomatoes and ham, and mix lightly. Add enough milk to make a soft dough.

3 Turn the dough onto a lightly floured surface, knead lightly, and roll out to an 8 x 6 in rectangle. Cut into 2 in squares, and arrange on the baking sheet.

4 Brush lightly with milk, sprinkle with paprika, and bake for 12–15 minutes. Transfer to a wire rack to cool.

NUTRITIONAL NOTES

PER PORTION:

CALORIES 113
FAT 4.23 g **SATURATED FAT** 0.65 g
CHOLESTEROL 2.98 mg **FIBER** 0.65 g

Granary Buns

These make excellent picnic fare, filled with cottage cheese, tuna, lettuce and low fat mayonnaise. They are also good served warm with soup.

Makes 8

NUTRITIONAL NOTES

PER PORTION:

CALORIES 223
FAT 1.14 g **SATURATED FAT** 0.16 g
CHOLESTEROL 0 **FIBER** 3.10 g

INGREDIENTS
1¼ cups warm water
1 tsp dried yeast
pinch of sugar
4 cups malted brown flour
1 tsp salt
1 tbsp malt extract
1 tbsp rolled oats

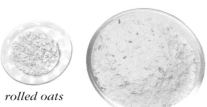

rolled oats

brown flour

water

malt extract

salt

dried yeast

VARIATION

To make a large loaf, shape the dough into a slightly flat round, and bake for about 30–40 minutes. Test it by tapping the base; if it sounds hollow, it is ready.

1 Put half the warm water in a small pitcher. Sprinkle in the yeast. Add the sugar, stir well, and let stand for 10 minutes.

2 Put the malted brown flour and salt in a mixing bowl, and make a well in the center. Add the yeast mixture with the malt extract and the remaining water. Gradually incorporate the flour, and mix to make a soft dough.

3 Turn the dough onto a floured surface, and knead for 5 minutes until smooth and elastic. Return to the clean bowl, cover with a damp dish towel, and let rise in a warm place for about 2 hours until doubled in bulk.

4 Lightly grease a large baking sheet. Turn the dough onto a floured surface, knead for 2 minutes, then divide into eight pieces. Shape into balls, and flatten with the palm of your hand to make neat 4 in rounds.

5 Place the rounds on the prepared baking sheet, cover loosely with a large plastic bag (ballooning it to trap the air inside), and let stand in a warm place until the buns are well risen. Preheat the oven to 425°F.

6 Brush the buns with water, sprinkle with the oats, and bake for about 20–25 minutes, or until they sound hollow when tapped underneath. Cool on a wire rack, then serve with the low fat filling of your choice.

Curry Crackers

These spicy, crisp little crackers are very low in fat and are ideal for serving with drinks.

Makes 12

INGREDIENTS
½ cup all-purpose flour
¼ tsp salt
1 tsp curry powder
¼ tsp chili powder
1 tbsp chopped fresh cilantro
2 tbsp water

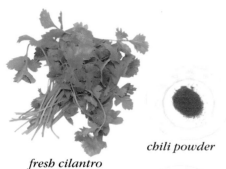

chili powder

fresh cilantro

salt

flour

water

curry powder

NUTRITIONAL NOTES
PER PORTION:

CALORIES 15
FAT 0.11 g **SATURATED FAT** 0.01 g
CHOLESTEROL 0 **FIBER** 0.21 g

1 Preheat the oven to 350°F. Sift together the flour and salt into a mixing bowl, then add the curry powder and chili powder. Make a well in the center, and add the chopped fresh cilantro and water. Gradually incorporate the flour, and mix to make a firm dough.

2 Turn onto a lightly floured surface, knead until smooth, then let rest for 5 minutes.

VARIATIONS
Omit the curry and chili powders, and add 1 tbsp caraway, fennel or mustard seeds.

3 Cut the dough into twelve pieces, and knead into small balls. Roll each ball out very thinly to a 4 in round.

4 Arrange the rounds on two ungreased baking sheets, then bake for 15 minutes, turning once during cooking. Cool on a wire rack.

Oat Cakes

Try serving these oat cakes with reduced-fat hard cheeses. They are also delicious topped with thick honey for breakfast.

Makes 8

INGREDIENTS
1 cup medium oatmeal, plus extra
    for sprinkling
½ tsp salt
pinch of baking soda
1 tbsp butter
5 tbsp water

medium oatmeal

baking soda   *salt*

water

butter

NUTRITIONAL NOTES
PER PORTION:

CALORIES 102
FAT 3.43 g **SATURATED FAT** 0.66 g
CHOLESTEROL 0.13 mg **FIBER** 1.49 g

COOK'S TIP
To achieve a neat round, place a 10 in plate on top of the oat cake. Cut away any excess dough with a knife, then remove the plate.

1 Preheat the oven to 300°F. Mix together the oatmeal, salt and baking soda in a mixing bowl.

2 Melt the butter with the water in a small saucepan. Bring to a boil, then add to the oatmeal mixture, and mix to make a moist dough.

3 Turn the dough onto a surface sprinkled with oatmeal, and knead to a smooth ball. Turn a large baking sheet upside down, grease it, sprinkle it lightly with oatmeal, and place the ball of dough on top. Sprinkle the dough with oatmeal, then roll out to a 10 in circle.

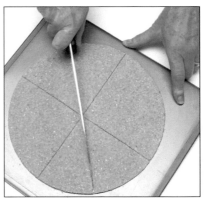

4 Cut the circle into eight sections, ease them apart slightly, and bake for about 50–60 minutes until crisp. Let cool on the baking sheet, then remove the oat cakes with a metal spatula.

Pancakes

These little pancakes are delicious with jam.

Makes 18

INGREDIENTS
2 cups self-rising flour
¹/₂ tsp salt
1 tbsp sugar
1 egg, beaten
1¹/₄ cups skim milk

egg

self-rising flour

salt

skim milk

sugar

1 Preheat a griddle or heavy-bottomed frying pan. Sift together the flour and salt into a mixing bowl. Stir in the sugar, and make a well in the center.

2 Add the egg and half the milk, then gradually incorporate the surrounding flour to make a smooth batter. Beat in the remaining milk.

NUTRITIONAL NOTES
PER PORTION:

CALORIES 64
FAT 1.09 g **SATURATED FAT** 0.20 g
CHOLESTEROL 11.03 mg **FIBER** 0.43 g

VARIATION

For a savory version of these scones, omit the sugar and add 2 chopped scallions and 1 tbsp freshly grated Parmesan cheese to the batter. Serve with cottage cheese.

3 Lightly grease the griddle or pan. Drop tablespoons of the batter onto the surface, leaving them until they bubble and the bubbles begin to burst.

4 Turn the pancakes over with a metal spatula, and cook until the bottoms are golden brown. Keep the cooked pancakes warm and moist by wrapping them in a clean napkin while cooking successive batches.

Pineapple and Cinnamon Pancakes

Making the batter with pineapple juice instead of milk cuts down on fat and adds to the flavor.

Makes 24

INGREDIENTS
1 cup self-rising whole-wheat flour
1 cup self-rising white flour
1 tsp ground cinnamon
1 tbsp sugar
1 large egg
1¼ cups pineapple juice
½ cup dried pineapple, chopped

dried pineapple

egg

pineapple juice

sugar

self-rising wholemeal flour

ground cinnamon

self-rising white flour

NUTRITIONAL NOTES

PER PORTION:

CALORIES 51
FAT 0.81 g **SATURATED FAT** 0.14 g
CHOLESTEROL 8.02 mg **FIBER** 0.76 g

1 Preheat a griddle or heavy-bottomed frying pan. Put the whole-wheat flour in a mixing bowl. Sift in the white flour, add the cinnamon and sugar, and make a well in the center.

2 Add the egg with half the pineapple juice, and gradually incorporate the surrounding flour to make a smooth batter. Beat in the remaining juice with the chopped pineapple.

COOK'S TIP

Pancakes don't keep well so are best eaten freshly cooked.

3 Lightly grease the griddle or pan. Drop tablespoons of the batter onto the surface, leaving them until they bubble and the bubbles begin to burst.

4 Turn the pancakes over with a metal spatula, and cook until the bottoms are golden brown. Keep the cooked pancakes warm and moist by wrapping them in a clean napkin while continuing to cook successive batches.

Soda Bread

Finding the bread box empty doesn't have to be a problem when your repertoire includes a recipe for soda bread. It takes just a few minutes to make and needs no rising or proving. If possible, eat soda bread while still warm from the oven – it does not keep well.

Serves 8

INGREDIENTS
4 cups all-purpose flour
1 tsp salt
1 tsp baking soda
1 tsp cream of tartar
1½ cups buttermilk

salt

buttermilk

baking soda

flour

cream of tartar

1 Preheat the oven to 425°F. Flour a baking sheet. Sift together all the dry ingredients into a mixing bowl, and make a well in the center.

COOK'S TIP

Soda bread needs a light hand. The ingredients should be bound together quickly in the bowl, and kneaded very briefly. The aim is just to get rid of the largest cracks, since the dough will become tough if it is handled too much.

2 Add the buttermilk, and stir quickly to make a soft dough. Turn onto a floured surface, and knead lightly. Shape into a round about 7 in in diameter, and place on the baking sheet.

3 Cut a deep cross into the top of the loaf, and sprinkle with a little flour. Bake for 25–30 minutes, then transfer the soda bread to a wire rack to cool.

NUTRITIONAL NOTES
PER PORTION:

CALORIES 230
FAT 1.03 g **SATURATED FAT** 0.24 g
CHOLESTEROL 0.88 mg **FIBER** 1.94 g

Prosciutto and Parmesan Bread

This nourishing bread is almost a meal in itself.

Serves 8

INGREDIENTS

2 cups self-rising whole-wheat
2 cups self-rising white flour
1 tsp baking powder
1 tsp salt
1 tsp freshly ground black pepper
3 oz prosciutto, chopped
2 tbsp freshly grated Parmesan
   cheese
2 tbsp chopped fresh parsley
3 tbsp French mustard
1½ cups buttermilk
skim milk, for glazing

1 Preheat the oven to 400°F. Flour a baking sheet. Place the whole-wheat flour in a bowl, and sift in the white flour, baking powder and salt. Add the pepper and the prosciutto. Reserve about 1 tbsp of the grated Parmesan, and stir the rest into the flour mixture. Stir in the parsley. Make a well in the center.

parsley
salt
Parmesan cheese
black pepper
self-rising white flour
self-rising whole-wheat flour
French mustard
buttermilk
prosciutto
baking powder

2 Mix the mustard and buttermilk in a pitcher, add to the flour mixture, and quickly mix to make a soft dough.

3 Turn the dough onto a floured surface, and knead briefly. Shape into an oval loaf, brush with milk, and sprinkle with the remaining cheese. Place the loaf on the prepared baking sheet.

4 Bake the loaf for 25–30 minutes, or until golden brown. Transfer to a wire rack to cool.

NUTRITIONAL NOTES

PER PORTION:

CALORIES 250
FAT 3.65 g **SATURATED FAT** 1.30 g
CHOLESTEROL 7.09 mg **FIBER** 3.81 g

Austrian Three Grain Bread

A mixture of grains gives this close-textured bread a delightful nutty flavor. Make two smaller twists, if preferred.

Serves 8–10

INGREDIENTS
2 cups warm water
2 tsp dried yeast
pinch of sugar
2 cups white bread flour
1½ tsp salt
2 cups malted brown flour
2 cups rye flour
2 tbsp linseed
½ cup medium oatmeal
3 tbsp sunflower seeds
2 tbsp malt extract

medium oatmeal

sunflower seeds

white bread flour

dried yeast

linseed

malt extract

water

rye flour

malted brown flour

salt

I Put half the water in a small pitcher. Sprinkle the yeast on top. Add the sugar, mix well, and let stand for 10 minutes.

2 Sift the white flour and salt into a mixing bowl, and add the other flours. Set aside 1 tsp of the linseed, and add the rest to the flour mixture with the oatmeal and sunflower seeds. Make a well in the center.

3 Add the yeast mixture to the bowl with the malt extract and the remaining water. Gradually incorporate the flour.

4 Mix to a soft dough, adding water, if necessary. Turn out onto a floured surface, and knead for about 5 minutes until smooth and elastic. Transfer to a clean bowl, cover with a damp dish towel, and let rise for about 2 hours until doubled in bulk.

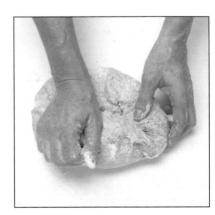

5 Flour a baking sheet. Turn the dough onto a floured surface, knead for 2 minutes, then divide in half. Roll each half into a 12 in cylinder.

6 Twist the two cylinders together, dampen the ends, and press to seal. Lift the twist onto the prepared baking sheet. Brush it with water, sprinkle with the remaining linseed, and cover loosely with a large plastic bag (ballooning it to trap the air inside). Let stand in a warm place until well risen. Preheat the oven to 425°F.

7 Bake the loaf for 10 minutes, then lower the oven temperature to 400°F, and cook for 20 minutes more, or until the loaf sounds hollow when it is tapped on the bottom. Transfer to a wire rack to cool.

NUTRITIONAL NOTES
Per portion:

CALORIES 367
FAT 5.36 g **SATURATED FAT** 0.60 g
CHOLESTEROL 0 **FIBER** 6.76 g

Banana and Cardamom Bread

The combination of banana and cardamom is delicious in this soft, moist loaf. It is a perfect afternoon snack with low fat spread and jam.

Serves 6

NUTRITIONAL NOTES
PER PORTION:

CALORIES 299
FAT 1.55 g **SATURATED FAT** 0.23 g
CHOLESTEROL 0 **FIBER** 2.65 g

COOK'S TIP
Make sure the bananas are really ripe, so that they give maximum flavor to the bread.

If you prefer, place the dough in one piece in a 9 x 3½ in loaf pan, and bake for an extra 5 minutes.

INGREDIENTS
⅔ cup warm water
1 tsp dried yeast
pinch of sugar
10 cardamom pods
3½ cups white bread flour
1 tsp salt
2 tbsp malt extract
2 ripe bananas, mashed
1 tsp sesame seeds

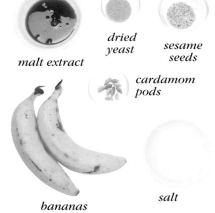

malt extract

dried yeast

sesame seeds

cardamom pods

bananas

salt

water

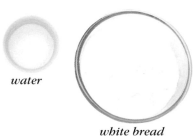

white bread flour

1 Put the water in a small bowl. Sprinkle the yeast on the top, add the sugar, and mix well. Let stand for 10 minutes.

2 Split the cardamom pods. Remove the seeds, and chop them finely.

3 Sift the flour and salt into a mixing bowl, and make a well in the center. Add the yeast mixture with the malt extract, chopped cardamom seeds and bananas.

4 Gradually incorporate the flour, and mix to make a soft dough, adding a little water, if necessary. Turn the dough onto a floured surface, and knead for about 5 minutes until smooth and elastic. Return to the clean bowl, cover with a damp dish towel, and let rise for about 2 hours until doubled in bulk.

5 Grease a baking sheet. Turn the dough onto a floured surface, knead briefly, then shape into a braid. Place the braid on the baking sheet, and cover loosely with a plastic bag (ballooning it to trap the air). Let stand until well risen. Preheat the oven to 425°F.

6 Brush the braid lightly with water, and sprinkle with the sesame seeds. Bake for 10 minutes, then lower the oven temperature to 400°F. Cook for 15 minutes more, or until the loaf sounds hollow when it is tapped on the bottom. Cool on a wire rack.

Golden Raisin Bread

A lightly sweetened bread that is delicious served warm. It is also excellent toasted and topped with a low fat spread.

NUTRITIONAL NOTES

PER PORTION:

CALORIES 273
FAT 4.86 g **SATURATED FAT** 0.57 g
CHOLESTEROL 0.39 mg **FIBER** 3.83 g

Serves 8–10

INGREDIENTS
²⁄₃ cup warm water
1 tsp dried yeast
1 tbsp honey
2 cups whole-wheat flour
2 cups white bread flour
1 tsp salt
²⁄₃ cup golden raisins
½ cup walnuts, chopped
¾ cup warm skim milk,
    plus extra for glazing

salt

white bread flour

walnuts

honey

water

skim milk

golden raisins

dried yeast
whole-wheat flour

VARIATION

To make Apple and Hazelnut Bread, replace the golden raisins with 2 chopped eating apples, and use chopped toasted hazelnuts instead of the walnuts. Add 1 tsp ground cinnamon with the flour.

1 Put the water in a small bowl. Sprinkle the yeast over the top. Add a few drops of the honey to help activate the yeast, stir well, and let stand for 10 minutes.

2 Put the flours in a bowl with the salt and golden raisins. Set aside 1 tbsp of the walnuts, and add the rest to the bowl. Mix together lightly, and make a well in the center.

3 Add the yeast mixture to the flour mixture with the milk and remaining honey. Gradually incorporate the flour, mixing to make a soft dough. Add a little water, if necessary.

4 Turn the dough onto a floured surface, and knead for 5 minutes until smooth and elastic. Return to the clean bowl, cover with a damp dish towel, and let rise in a warm place for about 2 hours, or until doubled in bulk. Grease a baking sheet.

5 Turn the dough onto a floured surface, and knead for 2 minutes, then shape into an 11 in long cylinder. Place the loaf on the prepared baking sheet. Make some diagonal cuts down the length of the loaf.

6 Brush the loaf with milk, sprinkle with the reserved walnuts, and let rise for about 40 minutes. Preheat the oven to 425°F. Bake the loaf for 10 minutes. Lower the oven temperature to 400°F, and bake for about 20 minutes more, or until the loaf sounds hollow when it is tapped on the bottom.

Rye Bread

Rye bread is popular in Northern Europe. It makes an excellent base for open sandwiches – add a low fat topping of your choice.

Makes 2 loaves, each serving 6

INGREDIENTS
2 cups warm water
2 tsp dried yeast
pinch of sugar
3 cups whole-wheat flour
2 cups rye flour
1 cup white bread flour
1½ tsp salt
2 tbsp caraway seeds
2 tbsp molasses
2 tbsp sunflower oil

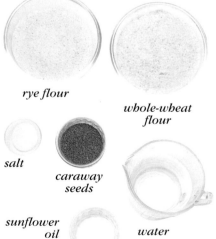

molasses
dried yeast
white bread flour

rye flour
whole-wheat flour

salt
caraway seeds

sunflower oil
water

1 Put half the water in a small pitcher. Sprinkle the yeast on top. Add the sugar, mix well, and let stand for 10 minutes.

2 Put the flours and salt in a bowl. Reserve 1 tsp of the caraway seeds, and add the rest to the bowl.

3 Make a well in the center of the flour mixture, then add the yeast mixture with the molasses, oil and the remaining water. Gradually incorporate the flour, and mix to make a soft dough, adding a little water, if necessary.

4 Turn the dough onto a floured surface, and knead for 5 minutes until smooth and elastic. Return to the clean bowl, cover with a damp dish towel, and let rise in a warm place for about 2 hours, or until doubled in bulk. Grease a baking sheet.

5 Turn the dough onto a floured surface and knead for 2 minutes, then divide the dough in half. Shape into two 9 in long ovals. Flatten the loaves slightly, and place them on the baking sheet.

6 Brush the loaves with water, and sprinkle with the remaining caraway seeds. Cover and let stand in a warm place for about 40 minutes until well risen. Preheat the oven to 400°F. Bake the loaves for 30 minutes, or until they sound hollow when they are tapped on the bottom. Cool on a wire rack. Serve the bread plain, or add a low fat topping of your choice.

NUTRITIONAL NOTES
Per portion:

CALORIES 224
FAT 3.43 g **SATURATED FAT** 0.33 g
CHOLESTEROL 0 **FIBER** 6.04 g

VARIATION
Shape the dough into two loaves, and bake in two greased 9 x 3½ in loaf pans, if you prefer.

Olive and Oregano Bread

This is an excellent accompaniment to all salads, and it is particularly good served warm.

NUTRITIONAL NOTES

PER PORTION:

CALORIES 202
FAT 3.28 g **SATURATED FAT** 0.46 g
CHOLESTEROL 0 **FIBER** 22.13 g

Serves 8–10

INGREDIENTS
1¼ cups warm water
1 tsp dried yeast
pinch of sugar
1 tbsp olive oil
1 onion, chopped
4 cups white bread flour
1 tsp salt
¼ tsp freshly ground black pepper
⅓ cup pitted black olives,
    coarsely chopped
1 tbsp black olive paste
1 tbsp chopped fresh oregano
1 tbsp chopped fresh parsley

fresh oregano   *fresh parsley*   *black olives*

white bread flour

black pepper

olive oil   *black olive paste*

water

dried yeast   *salt*   *onion*

1 Put half the warm water in a small pitcher. Sprinkle the yeast over the top. Add the sugar, mix well, and let stand for 10 minutes.

2 Heat the olive oil in a frying pan, and fry the onion until golden brown.

3 Sift the flour into a mixing bowl with the salt and pepper. Make a well in the center. Add the yeast mixture, the fried onion (with the oil), the olives, olive paste, herbs and remaining water. Gradually incorporate the flour, and mix to make a soft dough, adding a little more water, if necessary.

4 Turn the dough onto a floured surface, and knead for 5 minutes until smooth and elastic. Place in a clean bowl, cover with a damp dish towel, and let rise in a warm place for about 2 hours, or until doubled in bulk. Lightly grease a baking sheet.

5 Turn the dough onto a floured surface, and knead again for a few minutes. Shape into an 8 in round, and place on the prepared baking sheet. Using a sharp knife, make crisscross cuts over the top, cover, and let stand in a warm place for 30 minutes until well risen. Preheat the oven to 425°F.

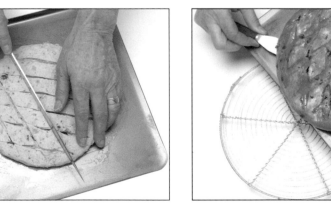

6 Dust the loaf with a little flour, and bake for 10 minutes. Lower the oven temperature to 400°F. Bake the loaf for 20 minutes more, or until it sounds hollow when it is tapped on the bottom. Transfer to a wire rack to cool slightly before serving.

Cheese and Onion Herb Sticks

A delicious bread that is very good with soup or salads. Use an extra-strong cheese to get plenty of flavor without piling on the fat.

Makes 2 sticks, each serving 4–6

INGREDIENTS
1¼ cups warm water
1 tsp dried yeast
pinch of sugar
1 tbsp sunflower oil
1 red onion, chopped
4 cups white bread flour
1 tsp salt
1 tsp dry mustard
3 tbsp chopped fresh herbs, such as thyme, parsley, marjoram or sage
¾ cup grated fat-reduced Cheddar cheese

fresh herbs

sunflower oil

fat-reduced Cheddar cheese

salt   *mustard*   *white bread flour*

water   *red onion dried yeast*

1 Put the water in a small pitcher. Sprinkle the yeast over the top. Add the sugar, mix well, and let stand for 10 minutes.

2 Heat the oil in a frying pan, and fry the onion until golden brown.

3 Sift the flour, salt and mustard into a mixing bowl. Add the herbs. Reserve 2 tbsp of the cheese. Stir the rest into the flour mixture, and make a well in the center. Add the yeast mixture with the fried onions and oil, then gradually incorporate the flour and mix to make a soft dough, adding water, if necessary.

4 Turn the dough onto a floured surface, and knead for 5 minutes until smooth and elastic. Return to the clean bowl, cover with a damp dish towel, and let rise in a warm place for about 2 hours, or until doubled in bulk. Lightly grease two baking sheets.

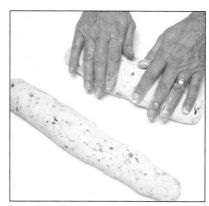

5 Turn the dough onto a floured surface, knead briefly, then divide the mixture in half. Roll each piece into a 12 in long stick. Place each stick on a baking sheet, and make diagonal cuts along the top.

NUTRITIONAL NOTES
PER PORTION:

CALORIES 210
FAT 3.16 g **SATURATED FAT** 0.25 g
CHOLESTEROL 3.22 mg **FIBER** 1.79 g

6 Sprinkle the sticks with the reserved cheese. Cover and let stand for about 30 minutes until well risen. Preheat the oven to 425°F. Bake the sticks for 25 minutes, or until they sound hollow when they are tapped on the bottom. Cool on a wire rack.

VARIATION
To make Onion and Coriander Sticks, omit the cheese, herbs and mustard. Add 1 tbsp ground coriander and 3 tbsp chopped, fresh cilantro instead.

Sun-dried Tomato Braid

This is a marvelous Mediterranean-flavored bread to serve at a summer buffet or barbecue.

Serves 8–10

INGREDIENTS

1¼ cups warm water
1 tsp dried yeast
pinch of sugar
2 cups whole-wheat flour
2 cups white bread flour
1 tsp salt
¼ tsp freshly ground black pepper
⅔ cup drained, oil packed sun-dried
  tomatoes chopped, plus 1 tbsp oil
  from the jar
¼ cup freshly grated Parmesan
  cheese
2 tbsp red pesto
1 tsp coarse sea salt

Parmesan cheese

red pesto

black pepper

whole-wheat flour

salt

dried yeast

sun-dried tomatoes

water

white bread flour

coarse sea salt

tomato oil

NUTRITIONAL NOTES

PER PORTION:

CALORIES 294
FAT 12.12 g **SATURATED FAT** 2.13 g
CHOLESTEROL 3.40 mg **FIBER** 3.39 g

COOK'S TIP

If you are unable to locate red pesto, use 2 tbsp chopped, fresh basil combined with 1 tbsp sun-dried tomato paste.

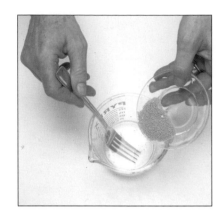

1 Put half the warm water in a small pitcher. Sprinkle the yeast over the top. Add the sugar, mix well, and let stand for 10 minutes.

2 Put the whole-wheat flour in a mixing bowl. Sift in the white flour, salt and pepper. Make a well in the center, and add the yeast mixture, sun-dried tomatoes, oil, Parmesan, pesto and the remaining water. Gradually incorporate the flour, and mix to make a soft dough, adding a little water, if necessary.

3 Turn the dough onto a floured surface, and knead for 5 minutes until smooth and elastic. Return to the clean bowl, cover with a damp dish towel, and let rise in a warm place for about 2 hours, or until doubled in bulk. Lightly grease a baking sheet.

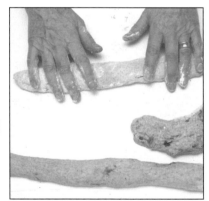

4 Turn the dough onto a lightly floured surface, and knead for a few minutes. Divide the dough into three equal pieces, and shape each one into a 13 in long cylinder.

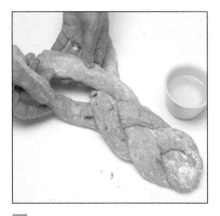

5 Dampen the ends of the three cylinders. Press them together at one end, braid them loosely, then press them together at the other end. Place on the baking sheet, cover, and let stand in a warm place for 30 minutes until well risen. Preheat the oven to 425°F.

6 Sprinkle the braid with the coarse sea salt. Bake for 10 minutes, then lower the oven temperature to 400°F, and bake for 15–20 minutes more, or until the loaf sounds hollow when tapped on the bottom. Cool on a wire rack.

Focaccia

This flat Italian bread is best served warm. It makes a delicious snack with low fat cheese and chunks of fresh tomato.

Serves 8

INGREDIENTS

1¼ cups warm water
1 tsp dried yeast
pinch of sugar
4 cups white bread flour
1 tsp salt
¼ tsp freshly ground black pepper
1 tbsp pesto
⅔ cup pitted black olives, chopped
3 tbsp drained, oil-packed sun-dried tomatoes, chopped, plus 1 tbsp oil from the jar
1 tsp coarse sea salt
1 tsp coarsely chopped fresh rosemary

1 Put the water in a bowl. Sprinkle the yeast over the top. Add the sugar, mix well, and let stand for 10 minutes. Lightly grease a 13 x 9 in jelly roll pan.

2 Sift the flour, salt and pepper into a bowl, and make a well in the center.

3 Add the yeast mixture with the pesto, olives and sun-dried tomatoes (reserve the oil). Mix to make a soft dough, adding a little water, if necessary.

black pepper

sun-dried tomatoes

pesto

white bread flour

black olives

coarse sea salt

salt

water

dried yeast

tomato oil

fresh rosemary

4 Turn the dough onto a floured surface, and knead for 5 minutes until smooth and elastic. Return to the clean bowl, cover with a damp dish towel, and let rise in a warm place for about 2 hours, or until doubled in bulk.

5 Turn the dough onto a floured surface, knead briefly, then roll out to a 13 x 9 in rectangle. Lift the dough over the rolling pin, and place in the prepared pan. Preheat the oven to 425°F.

 Using your fingertips, make small indentations all over the dough. Brush with the reserved oil from the sun-dried tomatoes, then sprinkle with the salt and rosemary. Let rise for 20 minutes, then bake for 20–25 minutes, or until golden. Transfer to a wire rack, but serve while still warm.

VARIATION
To make Oregano and Onion Focaccia, omit the pesto, olives and sun-dried tomatoes. Add 1 tbsp chopped, fresh oregano or 1 tsp dried oregano to the flour. Slice 1 onion very thinly into rounds, and scatter over the rolled-out dough. Drizzle with olive oil, and sprinkle with sea salt before baking.

Spinach and Bacon Bread

This bread is so tasty that it is a good idea to double the batch and freeze one of the loaves. Use smoked, lean back bacon for the best possible flavor with the minimum of fat.

NUTRITIONAL NOTES

PER PORTION:

CALORIES 172
FAT 2.17 g **SATURATED FAT** 0.36 g
CHOLESTEROL 1.97 mg **FIBER** 1.68 g

Makes 2 loaves, each serving 8

INGREDIENTS

2 cups warm water
2 tsp dried yeast
pinch of sugar
1 tbsp olive oil
1 onion, chopped
4 oz rindless smoked bacon rashers, chopped
8 oz chopped spinach, thawed if frozen
6 cups white bread flour
1½ tsp salt
½ tsp grated nutmeg
¼ cup grated fat-reduced Cheddar cheese

bacon rashers

dried yeast

grated nutmeg

olive oil

salt

fat-reduced Cheddar cheese

onion

water

white bread flour

spinach

1 Put the water in a small bowl. Sprinkle the yeast over the top, and add the sugar. Mix well, and let stand for 10 minutes. Grease two 9 in cake pans.

2 Heat the oil in a frying pan, and fry the onion and bacon for 10 minutes until golden brown. Meanwhile, if using frozen spinach, drain it thoroughly.

3 Sift the flour, salt and nutmeg into a mixing bowl, and make a well in the center. Add the yeast mixture. Add the fried bacon and onion (with the oil), then add the spinach. Gradually incorporate the flour mixture, and mix to make a soft dough.

4 Turn the dough onto a floured surface, and knead for 5 minutes until smooth and elastic. Return to the clean bowl, cover with a damp dish towel, and let rise in a warm place for about 2 hours, or until doubled in bulk.

COOK'S TIP

If using frozen spinach, be sure to squeeze out any excess liquid, or the resulting dough will be sticky.

5 Turn the dough onto a floured surface, knead briefly, then divide it in half. Shape each half into a ball, flatten slightly, and place in the pan, pressing the dough so that it extends to the edges. Mark each loaf into eight wedges, and sprinkle with the cheese. Cover loosely with a plastic bag, and let stand in a warm place until well risen. Preheat the oven to 400°F.

6 Bake the loaves for 25–30 minutes, or until they sound hollow when they are tapped on the bottom. Transfer to a wire rack to cool.

Malt Loaf

This is a rich and sticky loaf. If it lasts long enough to go stale, try toasting it for a delicious afternoon snack.

NUTRITIONAL NOTES

PER PORTION:

CALORIES 279
FAT 2.06 g **SATURATED FAT** 0.33 g
CHOLESTEROL 0.38 mg **FIBER** 1.79 g

Serves 8

INGREDIENTS
²/₃ cup warm skim milk
1 tsp dried yeast
pinch of sugar
3 cups all-purpose flour
¼ tsp salt
2 tbsp light brown sugar
generous 1 cup golden raisins
1 tbsp sunflower oil
3 tbsp malt extract

FOR THE GLAZE
2 tbsp sugar
2 tbsp water

golden raisins

malt extract

salt

flour

skim milk

light brown sugar

dried yeast

sunflower oil

1 Place the warm milk in a bowl. Sprinkle the yeast over the top, and add the sugar. Leave for 30 minutes until frothy. Sift the flour and salt into a mixing bowl, stir in the brown sugar and golden raisins, and make a well in the center.

2 Add the yeast mixture with the oil and malt extract. Gradually incorporate the flour, and mix to make a soft dough, adding a little milk, if necessary.

3 Turn onto a floured surface, and knead for about 5 minutes until smooth and elastic. Grease a 9 × 3½ in loaf pan.

4 Shape the dough, and place it in the prepared pan. Cover with a damp dish towel, and let stand in a warm place for 1–2 hours until well risen. Preheat the oven to 375°F.

5 Bake the loaf for 30–35 minutes, or until it sounds hollow when it is tapped on the bottom.

6 Meanwhile, prepare the glaze by dissolving the sugar in the water in a small pan. Bring to a boil, stirring, then lower the heat, and simmer for 1 minute. Place the loaf on a wire rack, and brush with the glaze while still hot. Let the loaf cool before serving.

VARIATION

To make buns, divide the dough into ten pieces, shape into rounds, let rise, then bake for 15–20 minutes. Brush with the glaze while still hot.

Cinnamon Apple Torte

Make this lovely cake for a fall celebration.

Serves 8

NUTRITIONAL NOTES

PER PORTION:

CALORIES 244
FAT 4.05 g **SATURATED FAT** 1.71 g
CHOLESTEROL 77.95 mg **FIBER** 1.50 g

INGREDIENTS
3 large eggs
½ cup superfine sugar
¾ cup all-purpose flour
1 tsp ground cinnamon

FOR THE FILLING AND TOPPING
4 large eating apples
4 tbsp honey
1 tbsp water
½ cup golden raisins
½ tsp ground cinnamon
1½ cups nonfat cream cheese
4 tbsp low fat ricotta cheese
2 tsp lemon juice
3 tbsp Apricot Glaze
mint sprigs, to decorate

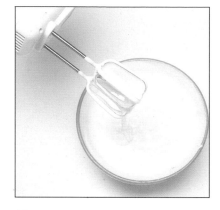

1 Preheat the oven to 375°F. Grease and line a 9 in spongecake pan. Place the eggs and sugar in a bowl, and beat with a hand-held electric mixer until thick and like a mousse (when the whisk is lifted, a trail should remain on the surface of the mixture for at least 15 seconds).

2 Sift the flour and cinnamon over the egg mixture, and carefully fold in with a large spoon. Pour into the prepared pan, and bake for 25–30 minutes, or until the cake springs back when lightly pressed. Slide a metal spatula between the cake and the pan to loosen the edge, then turn the cake onto a wire rack to cool.

3 To make the filling, peel, core and slice three of the apples, and put them in a saucepan. Add 2 tbsp of the honey and the water. Cover and cook over gentle heat for about 10 minutes, until the apples have softened. Add the golden raisins and cinnamon, stir well, replace the lid, and let cool.

eggs

eating apples

flour

low fat ricotta cheese

lemon

superfine sugar

golden raisins

Apricot Glaze

nonfat cream cheese

ground cinnamon

honey

4 Put the cream cheese in a bowl with the remaining honey, ricotta cheese and half the lemon juice. Beat until the mixture is smooth.

5 Halve the cake horizontally, place the bottom half on a board, and drizzle over any liquid from the apples. Spread with two-thirds of the cheese mixture, then top with the apple filling. Fit the top of the cake in place.

6 Swirl the remaining cheese mixture over the top of the cake. Core and slice the remaining apple, sprinkle with lemon juice, and use to decorate the edge of the cake. Brush the apple with warm Apricot Glaze, and decorate with a few mint sprigs.

Chestnut and Orange Roll

This moist cake is perfect to serve as a dessert.

Serves 8

NUTRITIONAL NOTES

PER PORTION:

CALORIES 185
FAT 4.01 g **SATURATED FAT** 1.47 g
CHOLESTEROL 76.25 mg **FIBER** 1.40 g

INGREDIENTS
3 large eggs, separated
¹/₂ cup superfine sugar
15¹/₂ oz can unsweetened
   chestnut purée
grated rind and juice of 1 orange
confectioner's sugar, for dusting

FOR THE FILLING
1 cup nonfat cream cheese
1 tbsp honey
1 orange

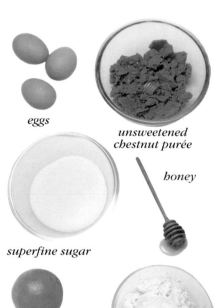

eggs

unsweetened chestnut purée

honey

superfine sugar

oranges

nonfat cream cheese

COOK'S TIP

Do not overbeat the egg whites, or you'll have trouble folding them into the mixture and they will form lumps in the roll.

1 Preheat the oven to 350°F. Grease a 12 x 8 in jelly roll pan, and line with parchment paper. Whisk the egg yolks and sugar in a bowl until thick.

2 Put the chestnut purée in a separate bowl. Whisk in the orange rind and juice, then whisk the flavored chestnut purée into the egg mixture.

3 Whisk the egg whites in a clean bowl until soft peaks form. Using a metal spoon, stir a generous spoonful of the whites into the chestnut mixture to lighten it, then fold in the rest.

4 Spoon the batter into the prepared pan, and bake for 30 minutes until firm. Cool for 5 minutes, then cover with a clean damp dish towel, and let stand until completely cold.

5 Meanwhile, make the filling. Put the cream cheese in a bowl with the honey. Finely grate the orange rind, and add to the bowl. Peel away all the pith from the orange, cut the fruit into segments, chop coarsely, and set aside. Add any juice to the cheese mixture, then beat until it is smooth. Stir in the chopped orange.

6 Sprinkle a sheet of waxed paper thickly with confectioner's sugar. Carefully turn the cake out onto the paper, then peel off the lining paper. Spread the filling over the cake, and roll it up like a jelly roll. Transfer to a plate, and dust with more confectioner's sugar.

Nectarine Amaretto Cake

Try this delicious cake with low fat ricotta cheese for dessert, or serve it solo for an afternoon snack. The syrup makes it moist but not soggy.

Serves 8

NUTRITIONAL NOTES

PER PORTION:

CALORIES 264
FAT 5.70 g **SATURATED FAT** 0.85 g
CHOLESTEROL 72.19 mg **FIBER** 1.08 g

INGREDIENTS
3 large eggs, separated
³/₄ cup superfine sugar
grated rind and juice of 1 lemon
¹/₃ cup semolina
¹/₃ cup ground almonds
¹/₄ cup all-purpose flour
2 nectarines or peaches, halved
and pitted
4 tbsp Apricot Glaze

FOR THE SYRUP
6 tbsp sugar
6 tbsp water
2 tbsp Amaretto liqueur

Amaretto liqueur

water

Apricot Glaze

eggs

semolina

superfine sugar

flour

lemon

ground almonds

nectarines

VARIATION
Use drained, canned mandarin orange segments for the topping, if desired, and use an orange-flavored liqueur instead of the Amaretto.

1 Preheat the oven to 350°F. Grease an 8 in round cake pan with a removable bottom. Whisk the egg yolks, sugar, lemon rind and juice in a bowl until thick, pale and creamy.

2 Fold in the semolina, almonds and flour until smooth.

3 Whisk the egg whites in a clean bowl until fairly stiff. Using a metal spoon, stir a generous spoonful of the whites into the semolina mixture to lighten it, then fold in the remaining egg whites. Spoon the mixture into the prepared cake pan.

4 Bake for 30–35 minutes, until the center of the cake springs back when lightly pressed. Remove the cake from the oven, and carefully loosen around the edge with a metal spatula. Prick the top of the cake with a skewer, and let cool slightly in the pan.

5 Meanwhile, make the syrup. Heat the sugar and water in a small pan, stirring until dissolved, then boil without stirring for 2 minutes. Add the Amaretto liqueur, and drizzle slowly over the cake.

6 Remove the cake from the pan, and transfer it to a serving plate. Slice the nectarines or peaches, arrange them over the top, and brush with the warm Apricot Glaze.

Strawberry Torte

It is hard to believe that this delicious gâteau is low in fat, but it is true, so enjoy!

Serves 6

INGREDIENTS
2 large eggs
6 tbsp superfine sugar
grated rind of ½ orange
½ cup all-purpose flour
strawberry leaves, to decorate
confectioner's sugar, for dusting
strawberry sauce, to serve (optional)

FOR THE FILLING
1¼ cups nonfat cream cheese
grated rind of ½ orange
2 tbsp superfine sugar
4 tbsp low fat ricotta cheese
8 oz strawberries, halved
¼ cup chopped almonds, toasted

NUTRITIONAL NOTES

PER PORTION:

CALORIES 213
FAT 6.08 g   SATURATED FAT 1.84 g
CHOLESTEROL 70.22 mg   FIBER 1.02 g

VARIATION
Use other soft fruits in season, such as currants, raspberries, blackberries or blueberries, or try a mixture of different berries.

low fat
ricotta cheese

eggs

strawberries

nonfat cream
cheese

almonds

superfine
sugar

orange

flour

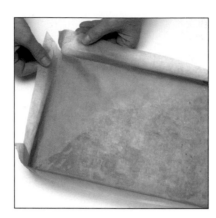

1 Preheat the oven to 375°F. Grease a 12 x 8 in jelly roll pan, and line it with parchment paper.

2 In a bowl, whisk the eggs, sugar and orange rind together with a hand-held electric mixer until thick and like a mousse (when the whisk is lifted, a trail should remain on the surface of the mixture for at least 15 seconds).

3 Fold in the flour with a metal spoon, being careful not to knock out any air. Turn into the prepared pan. Bake for 15–20 minutes, or until the cake springs back when lightly pressed. Turn the cake onto a wire rack, remove the parchment paper, and let cool.

4 Meanwhile, make the filling. In a bowl, mix the cream cheese with the orange rind, sugar and ricotta cheese until smooth. Divide between two bowls. Chop half the strawberry halves, and add to one bowl of filling.

5 Cut the cake widthwise into three equal pieces, and sandwich them together with the strawberry filling. Spread two-thirds of the plain filling over the sides of the cake, and press on the toasted almonds.

6 Spread the rest of the filling over the top of the cake, and decorate with the strawberry halves, and strawberry leaves, if liked. Dust with confectioner's sugar, and transfer to a serving platter. Serve with strawberry sauce, if you like.

Tia Maria Cake

A feather-light coffee sponge with a creamy liqueur-flavored filling.

Serves 8

INGREDIENTS
³/₄ cup all-purpose flour
2 tbsp instant coffee powder
3 large eggs
¹/₂ cup superfine sugar
coffee beans, to decorate (optional)

FOR THE FILLING
³/₄ cup nonfat cream cheese
1 tbsp honey
1 tbsp Tia Maria
¹/₄ cup preserved ginger, coarsely
   chopped

FOR THE ICING
1³/₄ cups confectioner's sugar, sifted
2 tsp coffee extract
1 tbsp water
1 tsp reduced-fat cocoa powder

NUTRITIONAL NOTES
PER PORTION:

CALORIES 226
FAT 3.14 g **SATURATED FAT** 1.17 g
CHOLESTEROL 75.03 mg **FIBER** 0.64 g

1 Preheat the oven to 375°F. Grease and line an 8 in deep round cake pan. Sift the flour and coffee powder together onto a sheet of waxed paper.

2 Whisk the eggs and sugar in a bowl with a hand-held electric mixer until thick and like a mousse (when the whisk is lifted, a trail should remain on the surface of the mixture for at least 15 seconds).

3 Gently fold in the flour mixture with a metal spoon, being careful not to knock out any air. Turn the mixture into the prepared pan. Bake the cake for 30–35 minutes, or until it springs back when lightly pressed. Turn onto a wire rack and leave to cool completely.

honey

eggs

coffee beans

coffee extract

nonfat cream cheese

coffee powder

preserved ginger

flour

icing sugar

superfine sugar

reduced-fat cocoa powder

Tia Maria

4 Make the filling. Mix the cream cheese with the honey in a bowl. Beat until smooth, then stir in the Tia Maria and chopped ginger.

5 Split the cake in half horizontally, and sandwich the two halves together with the Tia Maria filling.

6 Make the icing. In a bowl, mix the confectioner's sugar and coffee extract with enough of the water to make an icing that will coat the back of a wooden spoon. Pour three-quarters of the icing over the cake, spreading it evenly to the edges. Stir the cocoa into the remaining icing until smooth. Spoon into a pastry bag fitted with a writing tip, and pipe the mocha icing over the coffee icing. Decorate with coffee beans, if liked.

VARIATION
To make a Mocha Cake, replace the coffee powder with 2 tbsp reduced-fat cocoa powder, sifting it with the flour. Omit the ginger in the filling.

Raspberry Vacherin

Meringue rounds filled with orange-flavored ricotta cheese and fresh raspberries make a perfect dinner party dessert.

NUTRITIONAL NOTES
PER PORTION:

CALORIES 248
FAT 2.22 g SATURATED FAT 0.82 g
CHOLESTEROL 4.00 mg FIBER 1.06 g

Serves 6

INGREDIENTS
3 large egg whites
¾ cup superfine sugar
1 tsp chopped almonds
confectioner's sugar, for dusting
raspberry leaves, to decorate

FOR THE FILLING
¾ cup nonfat cream cheese
1–2 tbsp honey
1 tbsp Cointreau
½ cup low fat ricotta cheese
8 oz raspberries

honey

low fat ricotta cheese

raspberries

eggs

nonfat cream cheese

superfine sugar

chopped almonds

Cointreau

COOK'S TIP

When making the meringue, whisk the egg whites until they are so stiff that you can turn the bowl upside-down without them falling out.

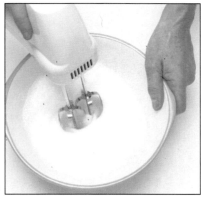

1 Preheat the oven to 275°F. Using a pencil, draw an 8 in circle on two pieces of parchment paper. Turn the paper over so that the marking is on the underside, and use it to line two heavy baking sheets.

2 Whisk the egg whites in a clean bowl until very stiff, then gradually whisk in the superfine sugar to make a stiff meringue mixture.

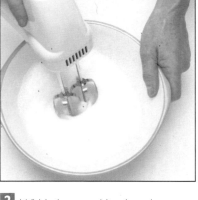

3 Spoon the mixture onto the circles on the prepared baking sheets, spreading the meringue evenly to the edges. Sprinkle one meringue round with the chopped almonds.

4 Bake for 1½–2 hours, then carefully lift the meringue rounds off the baking sheets, peel away the parchment paper, and cool on a wire rack.

5 To make the filling, combine the cream cheese with the honey and Cointreau in a bowl. Fold in the ricotta cheese and raspberries, reserving three of the best for decoration.

6 Place the plain meringue round on a board, spread with the filling, and top with the nut-covered round. Dust with confectioner's sugar, transfer to a serving platter, and decorate with the reserved raspberries, and a sprig of raspberry leaves, if liked.

Lemon Chiffon Cake

Lemon mousse provides a tangy filling for this
light lemon sponge.

Serves 8

INGREDIENTS
2 large eggs
6 tbsp superfine sugar
grated rind of 1 lemon
$\frac{1}{2}$ cup sifted all-purpose flour
Lemon Shreds, to decorate

FOR THE FILLING
2 eggs, separated
6 tbsp superfine sugar
grated rind and juice of 1 lemon
2 tbsp water
1 tbsp powdered gelatin
$\frac{1}{2}$ cup low fat ricotta cheese

FOR THE ICING
scant 1 cup confectioner's
    sugar, sifted
1 tbsp lemon juice

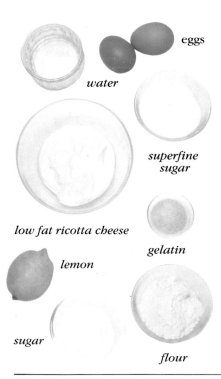

eggs

water

*superfine
sugar*

low fat ricotta cheese

gelatin

lemon

sugar

flour

1 Preheat the oven to 350°F. Grease
and line an 8 in cake pan with a
removable bottom. Whisk the eggs,
sugar and lemon rind together with a
hand-held electric mixer until thick and
like a mousse. Gently fold in the flour,
then turn the mixture into the pan.

2 Bake for 20–25 minutes, until the
cake springs back when lightly pressed in
the center. Turn onto a wire rack to
cool. Once cold, split the cake in half
horizontally, and return the lower half to
the clean cake pan. Set aside.

3 Make the filling. Place the egg yolks,
sugar, lemon rind and juice in a bowl.
Beat with a hand-held electric mixer until
thick, pale and creamy.

4 Pour the water into a small heat-
proof bowl, and sprinkle the gelatin on
top. Let stand until spongy, then place
over simmering water, and stir until
dissolved. Cool slightly, then whisk into
the yolk mixture. Fold in the ricotta
cheese. When the mixture begins to set,
quickly whisk the egg whites to soft
peaks. Fold a spoonful into the mousse
mixture to lighten it, then fold in the rest.

5 Pour the lemon mousse over the cake in the pan, spreading it to the edges. Set
the second layer of cake on top, and chill until set.

6 Slide a metal spatula dipped in hot water between the pan and the cake to loosen it, then carefully transfer the cake to a serving platter. Make the icing by adding enough lemon juice to the confectioner's sugar to make a mixture thick enough to coat the back of a wooden spoon. Pour over the cake, and spread evenly to the edges. Decorate with the Lemon Shreds.

NUTRITIONAL NOTES
PER PORTION:

CALORIES 202
FAT 2.81 g **SATURATED FAT** 0.79 g
CHOLESTEROL 96.41 mg **FIBER** 0.20 g

COOK'S TIP
The mousse mixture should be just on the point of setting when the egg whites are added. This setting process can be speeded up by placing the bowl of mousse in a bowl of iced water.

INDEX

A

Almonds:
  apricot and almond fingers, 33
  mango and amaretti
    strudel, 40
  nectarine Amaretto cake, 86
Amaretti cookies:
  filo and apricot purses, 26
  mango and amaretti strudel, 40
Amaretto liqueur:
  nectarine Amaretto cake, 86
Angel food cake, 42
Apples:
  apple and hazelnut bread, 66
  cinnamon apple torte, 82
  date and apple muffins, 31
  spiced apple cake, 47
Apricots:
  apricot and almond fingers, 33
  apricot glaze, 21
  banana and apricot Chelsea
    buns, 28
  filo and apricot purses, 26
  filo scrunchies, 27
Austrian three grain bread, 62

B

Bacon:
  spinach and bacon bread, 78
Baking pans, lining, 18
Bananas:
  banana and apricot Chelsea
    buns, 28
  banana and cardamom
    bread, 64
  banana and ginger quick
    bread, 46
  banana and golden raisin
    quick bread, 46
  banana gingerbread slices, 22
  chocolate banana cake, 38
Biscuits:
  chive and potato biscuits, 52
  ham and tomato biscuits, 53
Breads, 60–80
  apple and hazelnut bread, 66
  Austrian three grain bread, 62
  banana and cardamom
    bread, 64
  caraway bread sticks, 49
  cheese and onion herb
    sticks, 72
  coriander and sesame sticks, 49
  focaccia, 76
  golden raisin bread, 66
  granary buns, 54
  malt loaf, 80

  olive and oregano bread, 70
  onion and coriander sticks, 73
  oregano and onion focaccia, 77
  poppy seed rolls, 50
  prosciutto and Parmesan
    bread, 61
  rye bread, 68
  soda bread, 60
  spinach and bacon bread, 78
  sun-dried tomato braid, 74
Brown sugar meringues, 32
Buns:
  banana and apricot Chelsea
    buns, 28
  granary buns, 54

C

Caraway bread sticks, 49
Cardamom:
  banana and cardamom
    bread, 64
Cheese:
  cheese and onion herb
    sticks, 72
  prosciutto and Parmesan
    bread, 61
Chestnut and orange roll, 84
Chive and potato biscuits, 52
Chocolate:
  chocolate banana cake, 38
Cinnamon:
  cinnamon apple torte, 82
  pineapple and cinnamon
    pancakes, 59
Citrus fruits, 21
Coffee:
  coffee sponge drops, 34
  Tia Maria cake, 90
Coriander:
  coriander and sesame sticks, 49
  onion and coriander sticks, 73
Crackers:
  curry crackers, 56
  oat cakes, 57
  oaty crisps, 35
Curry crackers, 56

D

Dates:
  date and apple muffins, 31

spiced apple cake, 47

F

Filo pastry:
  filo and apricot purses, 26
  filo scrunchies, 27
Focaccia, 76
  oregano and onion focaccia, 77
Fruitcakes:
  fruit and nut cake, 37
  Irish whiskey cake, 36

G

Ginger:
  banana and ginger quick
    bread, 46
  banana gingerbread
    slices, 22
Golden raisin bread, 66
Granary buns, 54

H

Ham:
  ham and tomato biscuits, 53
Hazelnuts:
  apple and hazelnut bread, 66
Herb triangles, 48

I

Icing a cake, 20
Irish whiskey cake, 36

J

Jelly roll, peach, 44

L

Large cakes:
  angel food cake, 42
  chocolate banana cake, 38
  spiced apple cake, 47
  see also Fruitcakes; Jelly roll;
    Quick breads; Tortes
Lemon:
  lemon chiffon cake, 94
  lemon shreds, 21
  lemon sponge fingers, 24

M

Malt loaf, 80
Mango and amaretti strudel, 40
Meringues:
  brown sugar meringues, 32
  pineapple snowballs, 25
  raspberry vacherin, 92
Mocha cake, 91
Muffins:
  date and apple, 31

raspberry, 30

N

Nectarines:
  nectarine Amaretto cake, 86

O

Oats:
  oat cakes, 57
  oaty crisps, 35
Olive and oregano bread, 70
Onions:
  cheese and onion herb
    sticks, 72
  onion and coriander
    sticks, 73
  oregano and onion focaccia, 77
Orange:
  chestnut and orange roll, 84
  spicy orange fingers, 24
Oregano:
  olive and oregano bread, 70
  oregano and onion focaccia, 77

P

Pancakes, 58
  pineapple and cinnamon, 59
Pastries:
  filo and apricot purses, 26
  filo scrunchies, 27
Peaches:
  peach jelly roll, 44
Pear quick bread, 43
Pineapple:
  pineapple and cinnamon
    pancakes, 59
  pineapple snowballs, 25
Piping bag, making, 20
Poppy seed rolls, 50
Prosciutto: prosciutto and
    Parmesan bread, 61

Q

Quick breads:
  banana and ginger, 46
  banana and golden raisin, 46
  pear, 43

R

Raspberries:
  raspberry muffins, 30
  raspberry vacherin, 92
Roll, chestnut and orange, 84
Rolls:
  poppy seed rolls, 50
  shaping rolls, 17
Rye bread, 68

S

Sesame seeds:
  coriander and sesame sticks, 49
Snowballs, 25
Soda bread, 60
Spiced apple cake, 47
Spinach and bacon bread, 78
Sponge drops, coffee, 34
Sponge fingers:
  hazelnut, 24
  lemon, 24
Strawberry torte, 88
Strudel, mango and amaretti, 40
Sun-dried tomato braid, 74
Sun-dried tomato triangles, 48

T

Testing cakes, 19
Tia Maria cake, 90
Tomatoes:
  ham and tomato biscuits, 53
  sun-dried tomato braid, 74
  sun-dried tomato triangles, 48
Tortes:
  chestnut and orange roll, 84
  cinnamon apple torte, 82
  lemon chiffon cake, 94
  mocha cake, 91
  nectarine Amaretto cake, 86
  raspberry vacherin, 92
  strawberry torte, 88
  Tia Maria cake, 90

W

Whiskey:
  Irish whiskey cake, 36

Y

Yeast, 16, 51